WHAT PEOPLE SAY ABOUT NEIGHBOURHOOD PRAYER NETWORK

Prayer and action go hand in hand, and change people and communities. Through the work of Street Angels - CNI Network, we see week in and week out what happens when people pray for the wider community and follow this up with practical action - communities are made nicer, crime is reduced and lives are changed. We are thrilled to partner with Neighbourhood Prayer Network and hope that we will see a massive increase in Christians putting love into action, which will make our nation a different place!

Paul Blakey MBE
Founder, Street Angels - CNI Network / Love Your Streets.

I was very excited to hear about the Neighbourhood Prayer Project. God's timing is impeccable, as always. Here at Samaritan's Purse, we recently heard from one of our partners working in the Kibera slums in Kenya. Pastor Frank told us that individuals from his church were "taking personal charge" of the people and situations they were being confronted by every day, and he encouraged us to do the same: to "take charge." He reminded us of the power of intercessory prayer, lifting up in prayer people we know who are hurting or who are lost, people who need to experience something of God's love, His mercy and His grace. We were rightly moved to pray! We should all be praying for our communities, and I am very happy to endorse what the Neighbourhood Prayer Project is setting out to do. I just know that God will richly bless this initiative.

Brian Bennett
Head of Communications and International Ministry, Billy Graham Evangelistic Association, www.billygraham.org.uk.

As the Overseer of OSL and Renewal Christian Centre, we have embraced Neighbourhood Prayer as a vital part of our year of "Proclamation." Prayer has never been the last resort for Christians but rather the first and final solution for the cleansing and redeeming of our communities. I believe that this project will not only take Christ into our communities, but will open the doors for social as well as spiritual breakthrough. Prayer opens the door for us to walk through, it arranges opportunities, and it frees from strongholds. We are implementing Neighbourhood Prayer immediately after a town-wide outreach; we believe it will impact the streets and roads of Solihull.

Rt Rev. Dr David E. Carr
Overseer, www.orderofstleonard.org, www.renewalcc.org.

"Loving our neighbour" comes in all kinds of shapes and sizes. Praying for those I live next to has to play a vital part in seeing the Good News of Jesus brought to our communities.

Steve Clifford
General Director, Evangelical Alliance, www.eauk.org.

I am pleased to be supporting Neighbourhood Prayer Network. Church Edit works with churches across the UK, and I am excited to see how Neighbourhood Prayer Network will be used as a powerful prayer initiative, uniting churches across towns and the nation.

Kyle Cottington
Managing Director, Church Edit Websites, www.churchedit.co.uk.

We need to see our neighbourhoods in the way God sees them. Catching a vision for our community is always caught from prayer. I welcome this prayer initiative, which I am convinced will end with action and transformation.

Roy Crowne
Executive Director, www.hopetogether.org.uk.

I was absolutely thrilled when I heard about Neighbourhood Prayer Network. Not only is it a timely initiative, but it also highlights for us the pivotal and vital part that prayer makes in reaching our local community with the whole gospel. I wholeheartedly commend it.

John Glass
General Superintendent, Elim Churches, www.elim.org.uk.

I am convinced that prayer is a powerful first step in the process of community transformation. Part of our commission to love our neighbours is praying for them. I endorse this project and hope we have this in every neighbourhood.

Debra Green OBE
National Director, Redeeming Our Communities,
www.roc.uk.com.

All the evidence of history is that "more prayer" equals "more blessing." I can't wait to see the blessing that comes to neighbourhoods across our nation through this exciting new initiative.

Andy Hawthorne OBE
CEO, The Message Trust, www.message.org.uk.

It is good to welcome the Neighbourhood Prayer Network into the canopy of prayer that God is raising up to cover every person, every place and every sector of society. If each Christian did take up this invitation to simply pray and care for their neighbours, there would indeed be radical transformation in every community!

Jane Holloway
Prayer Director, World Prayer Centre, www.worldprayer.org.uk.

I gladly recommend Neighbourhood Prayer Network. God has for years been speaking to many folk about the importance of praying for our neighbours. As we do so, we shouldn't be surprised to see God answer prayer. He may even ask you to put feet on your prayers! I'm looking forward to hearing some of the stories of God at work through your prayers.

Brian Mills
Co-Founder, Interprayer, www.interprayer.com.

Neighbours, Transform YOUR street!

Bringing Prayer to our Neighbours, Bringing Community Back to our Streets

Rebekah Brettle
with Lyndall Bywater

Sovereign World

Sovereign World Ltd
PO Box 784
Ellel
Lancaster LA1 9DA
England

www.sovereignworld.com
www.facebook.com/sovereignworld
Twitter: @sovereignworld

ISBN 978 1 85240 713 1

The publishers aim to produce books which will help to extend and build up the Kingdom of God. We do not necessarily agree with every view expressed by the authors, or with every interpretation of Scripture expressed. We expect readers to make their own judgment in the light of their understanding of God's Word and in an attitude of Christian love and fellowship.

Editing by Mollie Barker
Design & Typesetting by David Lund. www.davidlunddesign.co.uk
Printed in the United Kingdom

Dedicated to...

The book is dedicated to all the men and women who have travelled to the UK from other nations and are helping spread the Gospel through our nation in a powerful way. Many of them work full time during the week, running churches in the evenings and at the weekend. Others work as part of church leadership teams, bringing with them a passion and testimony that enriches our churches across denominations. Others support the work of church projects, providing prayer and wisdom. We want to say "thank you," and also to say that we honour and appreciate you all!

Your efforts in this nation do not go unnoticed across the wider church. We want you to know our deep appreciation and that we do not underestimate the power of your prayers.

CONTENTS

LEGACY OF THE NATIONAL DAY OF PRAYER
WEMBLEY STADIUM
29 SEPTEMBER 2012

The National Day of Prayer aims to be a catalyst for ongoing mission and prayer. Neighbourhood Prayer Network, in partnership with Global Day of Prayer, London, has produced this guide with the intention of seeing the power of God impact every street in the United Kingdom. We hope that this will be the long-lasting legacy of this event and that the guide will be useful for five to ten years.

SPECIAL THANKS

SPECIAL THANKS

TO ALL INTERCESSORS

Neighbourhood Prayer Network would like to thank every single individual who prays, most often hidden from view, without anyone other than God knowing what you are doing or the hours you spend in prayer. This nation desperately needs your prayers! Thank you for all the prayers you have already prayed, and please continue to pray for our nation to be transformed through God's power.

Neighbourhood Prayer Network would like to extend special thanks to "Redeeming Our Communities." We would not exist if it wasn't for the inspiration of this charity and the friendship and support of Debra over the years. Whatever Neighbourhood Prayer Network achieves through God's grace, it will only be possible because of the tremendous foundation that Debra and her team have laid. Thank you.

DEBRA GREEN OBE
AND REDEEMING OUR COMMUNITIES

ROY CROWNE AND HOPE

Neighbourhood Prayer Network is keen to honour all the work that HOPE has done in both HOPE 08 and HOPE as they build to a year of mission in 2014 and beyond. We recognise the catalyst for unity that HOPE has been across the country, and indeed Neighbourhood Prayer Network has been influenced through past experience of working with HOPE in 2008. We would like to take this opportunity to endorse HOPE's literature and any future work. We pray that many using this guide will also turn to HOPE resources for inspiration.

in our villages, towns & cities

World Prayer Centre
BIRMINGHAM • ENGLAND

JANE HOLLOWAY
AND WORLD PRAYER CENTRE

Jane Holloway and the team at Prayer Forum and World Prayer Centre have worked tirelessly to build networks between prayer initiatives and to raise up prayer across the British Isles and beyond. We are aware that we stand on the foundations that you have laid and wish to honour all the prayer that has gone on in the years before. We are very grateful for your support and ongoing advice.

JONATHAN OLOYEDE
AND GLOBAL DAY OF PRAYER, LONDON

Neighbourhood Prayer Network would like to thank Jonathan and the Global Day of Prayer London team for all their efforts in working towards Wembley and other stadium events. The encouragement and opportunity provided help us in our vision of seeing every street in the UK covered in Christian prayer and encouraging people to reach out to their neighbours.

Thank you!

BRIAN MILLS

Special thanks to Brian Mills, who has mentored and encouraged so many people within the UK prayer movement and beyond. We also want to express our gratitude to him for his work in propagating prayer triplets.

CONTRIBUTORS AND NEIGHBOURHOOD PRAYER NETWORK TRUSTEES

Sincere thanks to all who have contributed to this guide through articles, prayer, advice and editing. Special thanks to Paul Stanier and the team at Sovereign World, to Mollie Barker for copy editing, to David Lund and Peter Seymour for designing the guide, and to my husband Carl Brettle. I am grateful to you all for your patience and effort in making this book a reality. Finally, thank you to the trustees - Sam Anim, Rev. Hilary Evans, Kyle Cottington, Jenny Bailey, Beverley Killa - for all their work in the background for Neighbourhood Prayer Network.

PREFACE

by Jonathan Oloyede

What you now hold in your hands is a miracle! Rebekah Brettle's team, and many others, sacrificed much to create this book. Therefore, I beg you, don't read it casually or with apathetic indifference. Browse it prayerfully with a thirsty heart and a hungry mind. Use it as a reference guide; send several copies to friends and colleagues; read it to your small groups, your congregation or your family. I believe that there is something unique in it for everyone. This manual could actually change your life permanently.

On 4 August 1991 I arrived back in the UK, where I was born, for a three-month holiday after medical school. The Lord then proceeded to interrupt my life plan, nudging me from medicine to ministry, and shifting my centre of cultural gravity from sunny tropical West Africa to cold grey Britain. Over the next ten years, the Holy Spirit visited me several times, with clear visions and dreams of what heaven was getting ready to do within the British Isles. The overriding message was, *"Unite and pray, church, so that God can transform our land."* The Lord showed me, in a vision, many groups praying the Lord's Prayer. They were of different sizes, made up of five, fifty, and 5,000 people. The smaller groups were the most numerous and covered every part of the British Isles.

As they prayed in sync, lights of fire were created above the praying groups, and those "balls of fire" were the same size, whether the people numbered five or 5,000. I then saw the whole of the Isles covered in a blazing light. As I observed, the Lord said, *"My people are already in place. Do not start anything new – join the dots."*

Another clear vision, which the Lord gave me years ago, was of crowds and crowds of young people coming out of everywhere, responding to the voice of God and forming an army. We believe that in this season, the younger generation will rise up in leadership. This is the time for trans-generational congregations, initiatives and movements; the young and old running together.

If you look around the Isles, in the major towns and cities, you will notice that the nations are here! I believe that within the bland, the bad and the beautiful of multicultural Britain lies the prophetic picture of God's will. The peoples of the world are here by God's mandate, to help the British Isles in this time of need. The good seeds planted by the missionary movement, centuries ago, have borne fruit. The seeds from that fruit have now returned to be a blessing.

From Wembley, we are commissioned to be His torch and light in every street, community and region within these Isles. This resource that you now hold in your hands helps us stay focused on the task, as we engage with our world at various levels of service and relationships. Keep it close; keep a copy in your office, home or car. Stay connected via the website for regular updates, as the Lord helps us join the dots and spawn a divine web of love and grace over the entire nation.

May His Kingdom come and His will be done on earth, in the British Isles, as it is in heaven.

Blessings and regards

Jonathan Oloyede
National Day of Prayer

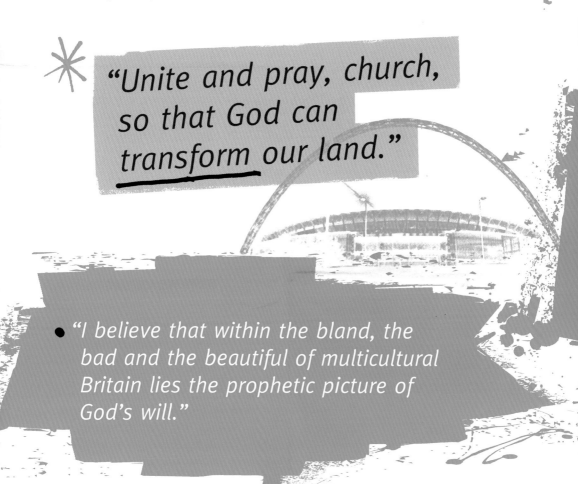

"Unite and pray, church, so that God can transform our land."

"I believe that within the bland, the bad and the beautiful of multicultural Britain lies the prophetic picture of God's will."

NEIGHBOURHOOD PRAYER NETWORK

AN INTRODUCTION TO NEIGHBOURHOOD PRAYER NETWORK by Rebekah Brettle

We have a vision to see every street in the United Kingdom covered in Christian prayer. We hope that Christians across the UK will take responsibility for praying for their own street and neighbours and getting to know their neighbours. In time, we also hope people will naturally begin to share their faith in Jesus. We believe this could transform the UK! This guide is designed to help individuals and churches, in partnership with similar ministries, to begin to see this vision realised.

Origins of the Vision

I first had part of the vision for Neighbourhood Prayer Network as an eight- or nine-year-old child, standing at my bedroom window one rainy afternoon. I

had a very close relationship with my grandmother, Edna Clapham, who often spoke about life in Britain in the days of World War Two and just afterward, when everyone knew everyone else and helped each other out. While the nightmare of that war was obviously something Grandma never wanted to return, she longed for the sense of community spirit in that time. As I looked out of the window, I gazed at the houses and the quiet working-class street; there was no one walking about. If it wasn't for the occasional light on in one or two houses, you could have been forgiven for thinking that no one lived there at all. The street felt empty and devoid of human activity. There was little or no community of the sort that Grandma spoke about with such fond memories. As I stared out of the window, I remember having a moment that I now, as an adult, understand as an experience of the Holy Spirit. In that quiet moment standing there, I knew God was going to use me in some way to change things.

Through my teenage years I lost my faith and became an atheist, finally coming back to Jesus on an Alpha course in 2003, after a long journey. The memory of that moment had never left me. I have felt like Jonah at times, running away from the enormity of the vision, feeling completely out of depth and tossed around by the storms of life. Now in my thirties, I can no longer escape the urge to fulfil what I feel God has asked me to do.

Loneliness and Quiet Desperation of Lives

I work as a GP two days per week. As a GP, I have the enormous privilege of observing people's lives – people from all backgrounds, all occupations and all faiths. It is genuinely heartbreaking to visit elderly people who are housebound (no longer able to leave the house due to illness or disability) and to know that, in some cases, I might be the only visitor they may get that month! There is an epidemic of loneliness and quiet desperation among all age groups across this nation. Our nation is one that is now desperate for the healing power and love of Jesus Christ.

In years gone by, we knew our neighbours, and in many streets across the UK that is still true. However, for the vast majority of people, few of us know our neighbours well, if we even know their names! It is staggering to realise that we live in an age when we communicate via Skype, Facebook or Twitter halfway across the earth; yet many of us, with our busy lives, have not found the time to get to know and care for those living on our own street! Please use this guide as an inspiration to get to know your neighbours, pray for your neighbours, and see your street transformed.

"I first had part of the vision for Neighbourhood Prayer Network as an eight- or nine-year-old child, standing at my bedroom window one rainy afternoon."

23

A HOUSE NEAR YOU...

HOUSE OF SICKNESS

HOUSE OF PRAYER

HOUSE OF CAPTIVITY

HOUSE OF BLESSING

HOUSE OF GRIEF

HOUSE OF HOPE

HOUSE OF DESPAIR

HOUSE OF HEALING

HOUSE OF FAITH

HOUSE OF FEAR

HOUSE OF LONELINESS

HOUSE OF HOSPITALITY

HOUSE OF REJECTION

HOUSE OF LOVE

Neighbourhood Prayer Network works on a principle of praying for our neighbours, caring for our neighbours and, when the opportunity arises (and only if you have prayed and cared), sharing the gospel with your neighbours. We do not claim to offer anything new, except to focus efforts on those living nearest to us, in our own streets. We build on the foundations of many existing prayer initiatives and with the intention of forming partnerships with anyone who shares our vision.

We hope, in this section, to show you why your street desperately needs your prayers.

Our logo shows three houses. The middle one is a Christian home that prays and, as it does so, the light spreads to the other houses.

In the beginning, we do not expect you to pray for every house on your street; that would be overwhelming. But we hope you will start praying for three households on your street. We have written several prayer guides to help you, which appear in the chapter headed "Prayer" (page 92). One of these is the "Neighbourhood Prayer Triplets" guide, again linking back to our logo. We hope you will join with two other Christians from other streets near you, to pray together regularly.

Jesus says,

> You are the light of the world. A city that is set on a hill cannot be hidden. Nor do they light a lamp and put it under a basket, but on a lampstand, and it gives light to all who are in the house. Let your light so shine before men, that they may see your good works and glorify your Father in heaven.
> (Matthew 5:14–16)

Lighthouses of Prayer

To all the houses praying for their neighbours we are giving the title "Lighthouses of Prayer," partly because Pray for Scotland, one of our partners, uses this name for a similar initiative and partly because there are other groups called "Lighthouses" praying already for their neighbours in other parts

"Could your home become a Lighthouse for your street?"

of the country, such as Norwich and Essex. Neighbourhood Prayer Network would prefer people living in Scotland to please contact Pray for Scotland.

Avril Betts-Brown, who co-ordinates a network of Lighthouses of Prayer in Essex, hopes to work with us in the near future. She told me that during a prayer meeting the group felt that God had said the following:

- *"Lighthouses take a lot of flak, have to be incredibly strong structures, and take a great deal of effort and time to build, but they are worth it because they direct people away from danger and onto the right way."*
- *"Lighthouses are like an underground central heating system, secretly warming up the area with the Holy Spirit, keeping everything warm so the area doesn't become cold and hard."*

We hope to join the prayer that is already taking place, celebrating both what has gone before and also what is already happening. Could your home become a Lighthouse for your street?

National Statistics or the People Behind the Doors?

In this section, we have chosen not to bombard you with statistics, trying instead to present in a creative way the types of problems you might find behind doors on your street. We have deliberately drawn a contrast between houses in difficulty and a typical Christian house offering prayer, care and God's love. We have provided some statistics in our Neighbourhood Prayer Diary on page 153. We also recommend *Operation World* (seventh edition) by Jason Mandryk, which provides statistics and prayer points about the UK and all other nations.

Caution: Any activity that involves getting to know adult neighbours is not suitable for children. While the vast majority of people will never harm a child, Neighbourhood Prayer Network is concerned that there are individuals who may abuse a child's trust and harm a child. We ask parents with children to be vigilant about this risk.

House of sickness

In your street, in every street, there are people who live every day with illness and pain. Some have physical illnesses that they have had since birth, blindness, deafness, autism or other disabilities. Others are sick because they have cancer, arthritis, back pain, diabetes. Some you wouldn't even know were ill, for they look OK; they put on a brave face and hide their pain.

Many other people have depression and anxiety or mental illnesses – much more common than many of us realise – but, because of the stigma attached to these conditions, they often hide their illness from their friends and family. Yet others have suffered a trauma in their lives, including rejection, abuse or an accident, and need emotional healing.

With a rising elderly population, every street in the UK will have someone struggling with illness, or a family affected by illness.

House of healing

And He came down with them and stood on a level place with a crowd of His disciples and a great multitude of people from all Judea and Jerusalem, and from the seacoast of Tyre and Sidon, who came to hear Him and be healed of their diseases, as well as those who were tormented with unclean spirits. And they were healed. And the whole multitude sought to touch Him, for power went out from Him and healed them all.
(Luke 6:17–19)

We may focus on physical healing, but people often have other areas of their lives that need healing. Sometimes the most powerful part you can play in someone's healing is simply to show them love. Never underestimate the power of love! Below are four aspects of healing:

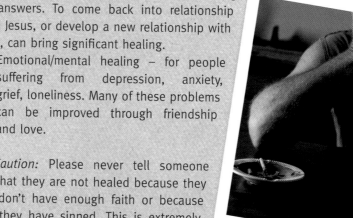

- Physical healing – for those suffering from blindness, deafness, infertility, a broken bone, cancer, arthritis, etc. (See the articles "Healing on the Streets" on page 186 and "CAP" on page 174.)
- Social healing – for the lonely person, the rejected person, the person with few friends. To find a sense of community and friendship can be extremely healing for many people.
- Spiritual healing – for the person struggling with guilt, the person who may have been a Christian in the past but is angry with God, and those searching for answers. To come back into relationship with Jesus, or develop a new relationship with Him, can bring significant healing.

- Emotional/mental healing – for people suffering from depression, anxiety, grief, loneliness. Many of these problems can be improved through friendship and love.

Caution: Please never tell someone that they are not healed because they don't have enough faith or because they have sinned. This is extremely damaging and can become a future barrier to faith and healing.

Prayer

- Pray for those living on your street who may be suffering from illness, that their illness does not get any worse.
- Pray for those in physical or psychological pain, that there would be an improvement.
- Pray for medical staff looking after people, that they will always act in compassion.
- Pray for finances.
- Pray for friends to not tire of visiting.
- Pray for the wider family, that they will be brought closer and not separated by illness.

Care

- If your neighbour has recently become unwell, could you send them a "get well" card, or buy them some flowers?
- Can you help them with shopping, or cook some food for them while they are unwell?
- Can you visit them with a friend, for the time that they are unwell? If this is a long-term illness, can you keep this up? You should ideally do this in twos unless you know the person very well. If your neighbour doesn't want you to visit, please respect their privacy.
- Could you take your neighbour to hospital appointments?

Share (if you know your neighbour well)

- Could you tell your neighbour that you are praying for them and that you believe that God can help them?
- At Christmas or Easter, could you give them the Father's Love Letter? (See page 218.)
- At Christmas can you send them a Christmas card and invite them to your church's carol service?
- As you get to know them well, can you tell them about your life and how God has helped you?

House of fear

Many people across the country have been victims of crime, such as being physically assaulted, raped, burgled, mugged, bullied and threatened, or they are suffering from the antisocial behaviour of neighbours. Perhaps they have been a victim of racism or discrimination, or they live alone, having never personally had anything happen to them but fearing that something will happen in the future.

Others fear losing a loved one, their job, their relationships, or are facing an incredibly difficult situation in their family. Others fear becoming unwell and death itself. Fear is the opposite of faith.

House of faith

Prayer

- Pray for God's will to be done in your street.
- Pray for faith to replace fear in your life and in your neighbours' lives.
- Pray for your local neighbourhood policing officers.
- Look on the website www.police.uk for crime rates in your area, praying strategically for crime to reduce or for future crime not to occur.
- Pray for all people who are victims of domestic violence, both male and female.
- Pray for racism and prejudice to disappear on your street.
- Pray for protection from violence, bullying and burglary, for all those living on your street.

Care

- Can you send your Neighbourhood Police Officer a "thank you" card for the work they do and offer your home as a place to stop for tea? Visit the Christian Police Association website for additional guidelines (www.cpauk.net).
- Is there someone from another culture living on your street? Could you and your family befriend them and get to know them?
- If you know that someone has been a victim of crime, could you help them in some way as God leads?
- Could you set up a local Neighbourhood Watch for your street? This is a national organisation with strong links to the police (www.neighbourhoodwatch.net). It is not a Christian organisation, but it is an opportunity to care for your neighbours, and get to know them and their situations, allowing you to pray for them more effectively. (See the article "Ballymena House of Prayer" on page 88.)

Share (with neighbours you know well)

- If you have been through a similar situation or a difficult situation and God helped you through it, if you feel able or that it is appropriate, share this with your neighbour.

- Could you share with your local Neighbourhood Police Officer some of the crime reduction stories that have happened as people have prayed? For more information on some of the stories listed in this guide, visit Redeeming Our Communities (www.roc.uk.com) or the Christian Police Association (www.cpauk.net).

House of loneliness

Many people today are excluded from society. Maybe they are elderly and are afraid of falling if they leave the house; their families no longer live nearby so they spend day after day living inside their house, with few visitors except maybe the district nurse or the postman. Some are not even that lucky.

Asylum seekers are often made to feel they are not welcome. The UK government may already have moved them several times, which makes it difficult for them to form meaningful friendships, and the money they are given – contrary to what the media tells us – is barely enough to survive. There may be an asylum seeker on your street who fled to the UK after seeing members of their family arrested and tortured or even killed. It doesn't matter that they are a genuine case – no one seems to believe them. They may find English hard to understand.

A single mother or father works hard to pay the bills, raise their child, and in some cases has little time for much else. Many lone parents have seen marriages and relationships fail and are left facing middle age living on their own.

House of hospitality

Prayer
- Pray for all people feeling lonely, that they will know God's presence in their life.
- Pray for all of the elderly living on our streets, that they will find community where they live.
- Pray for the asylum seekers, single-parent families and those going through relationship breakdown, that they will feel loved and accepted where they live.
- Pray especially at Christmas, birthdays, Easter and family occasions, that the lonely will have genuine friends who care for them.

Care

- Is there someone on your street who never goes out or you rarely see have visitors?
- Could you, with someone else, visit them to check they are OK?
- Could you get to know them, invite them round for a meal?
- At Christmas time, if someone on your street has nowhere to spend Christmas, would you be willing to invite them round to your house, even if it was only for an hour or so, or could you visit them?
- Could you gather together several people for a regular afternoon tea every fortnight?
- Could you help the elderly person with their shopping, gardening, household chores?
- Could you visit a nursing home with your church and seek out the people who have no visitors?
- Could you send them Christmas cards, birthday presents, etc?
- Could you befriend an asylum seeker and introduce them to friends from church?

Share
- Let your life show Jesus to your neighbour.
- Be willing to answer questions about your faith if your neighbour asks, and invite them to church if God leads you. The time is not always the right one, so listen to God.

House of rejection

There are people who have been rejected by their family because they were from a culture where they were supposed to marry someone their family suggested. Rejecting this arranged marriage has meant exclusion from their wider family.

Others were abused when they were children and ran away. They don't trust people and often try to raise their children in isolation.

Some children have fathers or mothers who don't spend time with them. They wait patiently to hear from Mum or Dad, but that birthday card never comes, the promised trip at the weekend never materialises. Still others came to love a stepfather or stepmother, only to have them too leave the house when yet another relationship broke down.

Others have been rejected in later life by family, partners, daughters or sons, and every birthday, every Christmas, every family celebration is a reminder of rejection, bringing great pain.

House of love

Prayer

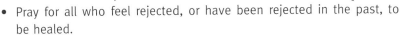

- Pray that all who feel rejected will come to know God as a loving Father who will never leave them or forsake them.
- Pray that they will one day find acceptance in a loving Christian community and that, even if they never become a Christian, they will always feel loved by Christians.
- Pray for reconciliation where possible between members of families, but protection from abuse if there has been past abuse.
- Pray for all who feel rejected, or have been rejected in the past, to be healed.
- Pray for protection from feelings of self-harm, suicide and depression.
- Pray for strong friendship and community to surround them.

Care

- Invite those who feel rejected round to a meal, or go out for a coffee or similar.
- In the case of children, try to befriend the family as a whole; never put yourself in a position where you are on your own with a child other than your own relatives.
- Make sure you remember your neighbour at difficult times of the year: Christmas, Easter, birthdays, anniversaries or times when people gather.
- If you have spare clothes or furniture that you are getting rid of, ask your neighbours if they need any of it before throwing it away. (See page 182 for the article "Acts 435: Now We're All Neighbours.")
- Give encouraging words; invite them to join a street Facebook page or your own account.
- Cook food, if appropriate, and take it round to their house.
- Ask God to show you how you can show love to your neighbour.

Share (for neighbours you now know)
- Invite your neighbour to your church barbecue, your carol service, church social functions.
- Share your testimony with them if it comes up in conversation.
- Live your life in a way that your love for others shines through.
- Invite them to an Alpha course or similar (see page 221 for the article "Alpha").
- Send them the Father's Love Letter as a gift (see page 218).

House of despair

Perhaps living on your street there are families struggling under a mountain of debt. Every day they fear the post, for it brings another red letter, reminding them that they are unable to pay the bill and will face consequences. Other envelopes are from companies that have given them payday loans, taking advantage of their desperate situation. With several children to feed, a single mother misses a meal.

In another household, there is a woman who has been trafficked, brought to the UK with the promise of a better life; instead she has been led into a life of prostitution and slavery. She lives in fear of the people who brought her. She feels nobody can help her.

- See page 189 for the article "Human Trafficking".
- See page 174 for the article "CAP".
- See page 183 for the article "Foodbank, Newham".

House of hope

Prayer

- Pray for all those living with considerable debts, that they will not fall victim to worsening debts, through payday loans or loan sharks.
- Pray for all who are struggling to pay bills because of debts, unemployment, illness or simply because the cost of living is rising.
- Pray for all children who may be living on your street who are not eating a balanced diet because of lack of money to buy food. Recent reports have shown a rise in the number of children who are hungry at school. (See the article "Foodbank, Newham" on page 183.)
- Pray for resolution of debt problems in families and enough money for people to meet their bills.
- Pray for employment in jobs that will allow them to provide for their families. Where ill health prevents work, pray for an improvement in health.

Care

- Could you donate furniture or clothes to a family in need on your street, or if you are lucky enough to live on an affluent street, could you donate through ACTS 435? (See the article on page 182.)
- Could you recommend CAP (Christians Against Poverty) to a neighbour struggling with debt? Or could your church run a CAP Money course? If one doesn't exist, perhaps you could set one up. (See the article on page 174.)
- Could you donate money to a local foodbank, or if one doesn't exist and there is a need in your area, could you set one up? (See the article on page 183.)
- Can you keep your eyes open for people who may be victims of trafficking? This trade – modern-day slavery – can only continue as long as people are blind to what goes on around them. Report suspicions to Crimestoppers (www.crimestoppers-uk.org) if you are concerned.
- Can you just generally love your neighbour in difficulty, be a friend, be a good neighbour, treat people as you would like to be treated?

Share

- Show your neighbour so much love that they have no option but to ask why you are different from others.
- Be prepared to answer questions about your faith, if they ask.
- Can you invite your neighbour to events your local church puts on?

House of grief

This is a household where a husband has lost a wife, or a wife a husband, where a child has died, years before their time, where a miscarriage has taken place, where a road traffic accident or cancer has robbed someone of a loved one. This is a house of sorrow.

House of blessing

Prayer

- Pray for your neighbour to be comforted. "Blessed are those who mourn, for they shall be comforted" (Matthew 5:4).
- Pray for protection for people from feelings of self-harm and suicide.
- Pray for them to have family and friends who are supportive.
- Pray for the months and years later, when everyone feels they should have moved on, but they still struggle with the loss.
- Pray that they will come to know God as a Father who cares for them and will never leave them or forsake them.

Care

- Send them a card, saying that you are sorry to hear about their loss. Remember the time that their loved one died and remember a year later to check they are OK.
- Send food round if they are on their own, or invite them to your home for a meal.
- Invite them to social events, such as tea parties for other neighbours, or to church events.
- If you can afford it, treat them to a trip to the theatre, cinema etc.

Share

- Give them the Father's Love Letter if you feel it is appropriate (see page 218).
- Attend a funeral if you are able.
- Invite them to church.
- Share your story of what God has done in your life.
- Be willing to answer questions about your faith if they ask.
- Keep praying for them and let them know you are praying.

House of captivity

Many people live as slaves to the latest model of smartphone, or whatever their money can buy each week. Games, parties, drink and drugs can't seem to fill the void in their lives. They have tried New Age religions, psychics, reiki, etc., and yet they have not found what they are looking for. They get drunk at the weekends; they have sex with multiple people each year.

Some have turned to alcohol, to smoking, to drugs, to overeating, to buying as much as they can each week. They are searching for answers to what they need to fill the void, yet they don't know what it is. They do not know God.

House of prayer

- Pray for all people living in your street who do not yet know Jesus, that they will come to know Him.
- Pray for all who profess to be Christian but, for whatever reason, no longer attend church.
- Pray for those with blinded eyes to see the truth clearly.
- Pray for the local churches to work together, to reach out to your neighbours in prayer, love and in sharing the gospel.
- Pray for a complete transformation of their lives and healing from the past.
- Pray for the Holy Spirit to visit your street in power and for local churches to be ready.

Care

Live a life that testifies to your faith; be a good neighbour. If someone moves into your street, be the first to welcome them. If someone has a new baby, be the first to send a card and if possible a present. Aim to create a street where everyone is friendly to one another.

Share

Ideally form a prayer triplet and follow some of the ideas in this guide. People from your church who do not live on your street are sometimes better equipped to give out prayer request cards, or the Father's Love Letter. (See page 218.)

Remember, nobody will listen to you unless your lifestyle is one of genuine love, and believe me (writes Rebekah), having been a non-Christian for many years, they know the difference. It was often how people treated me and others that made me decide if I would pay any attention to them. Equally, it was when I was badly treated by a Christian that I took a step further away from God. How you live your life is much more important than what you say!

"HOW TO" GUIDE

Neighbourhood
PRAYER.NET

Starting Neighbourhood Prayer in Your Street

We aim eventually to have a map of every street in the UK and to highlight which streets are being prayed for. It is helpful to us if you could let us know if you are praying for your street, so that we do not duplicate the work of our partners and similar ministries. In the future, areas where there are few people praying will be targeted strategically. In this early stage, we want to start gathering data about which streets are praying.

As an individual

- Please register your street and your name with our website. We hope eventually to produce a street-level map showing streets where prayer is taking place. We will be working closely with Pray for Scotland, Adopt a Street / Street Pastors, and similar projects in this regard.
- Aim initially to pray for three households on your street, at least once a week.
- Please inform your church leader about what you are doing and give feedback to your church relating to your experiences.
- Encourage at least two others to start praying for their street, and consider forming a prayer triplet (see page 98).

Prayer

We have provided several prayer guides to help you start praying. Wendy Thomas is encouraging everyone to pray a blessing over their street as part of Adopt a Street / Street Pastors. We strongly support this idea. We have a prayer-walk guide based around blessing on page 162. For stories of transformation related to praying blessing, see the articles "Ffald-y-Brenin" on page 58; and "Riding the Wave, Belfast" on page 85.

- We produce Friday prayers, called "Neighbour Fridays," in *Prayer for Today*, a UCB publication. To receive this publication, please contact www.ucb.co.uk/prayerfortoday.
- We also have prayer guides entitled "Neighbourhood Prayer Diary," produced in partnership with Tearfund, and "Forty Days of Prayer" (see pages 153 and 124).

Care

We are asking people to get to know their neighbours. The prayer guides provide prayer challenges to facilitate this and there are ideas for outreach to your neighbours in the yearly diary section, produced in partnership with other charities.

Share

We realise that not everyone is comfortable in sharing their faith with neighbours, but we hope as you genuinely pray and love your neighbours that they will start to ask questions about your life. We believe that many of this country's problems could be significantly reduced if more people came into relationship with Jesus. Please see the chapter "Share," on evangelism, which was written to help people who want to share their faith to do so. However, we wish to stress that we believe you should only share your faith if you have been praying for and getting to know people over a period of time. It should also be done out of a place of love and compassion, and we are keen to point out that Jesus asked us not to get people to make decisions to believe, but to make disciples. Sometimes people become disciples before they believe! Equally, after someone believes, they need to become a disciple who follows Jesus' teachings.

As a small group or a home group

Please register with the www.neighbourhoodprayer.net website and list all the streets that you are praying for.

Prayer

We have several prayer guides as listed:

- "Neighbourhood Prayer Triplets"
- "Forty Days of Prayer"
    - "Neighbourhood Prayer Diary"
    - "Planning a Prayer Walk to Bless Your Neighbourhood"
    - "Neighbour Fridays"

Neighbourhood Prayer Triplets: We are hoping that people will form prayer triplets representing three different streets. These prayer triplets most often will be made up of people from your own church; however, if you live a long way from your church you may want to pray with Christians living nearby, from another church. We have produced a prayer triplet guide (see page 98), particularly for those who don't normally go to a prayer meeting. We hope that this twelve-week guide will help teach on prayer, using Scripture, and allow new groups to grow in confidence. Prayer triplets are powerful and have a fairly long history over the last few years. These triplets are designed specifically for your neighbours and for your streets.

Care

You may be able to join together with others from your church or home groups to put on a barbecue, visit the elderly or people in difficulty, or do some DIY jobs for your community. Perhaps hold a street party or, in June, invite someone to the "Big Lunch" (see the Diary of the Year on page 224).

Share

You could deliver prayer request cards to multiple streets, asking your neighbours what they would like you to pray for (see page 169 for a sample prayer request card). The idea behind this is that you agree to pray for your neighbours for two weeks; the cards are either collected or sent to your local church. This often opens up opportunities to get to know people, especially if done regularly over a few years. Please ensure that your church leadership is aware of what you are doing.

You could deliver newspapers at Easter (see the article "Real News" on page 81) or the Father's Love Letter (see page 218) or put on a local Alpha course in a home in your neighbourhood (see page 221).

Churches

We are aware of the incredible amount of prayer walking and prayer that already goes on in many churches.

We are hoping we can find church partners and that these partners will help motivate their congregations to pray for their streets. We believe that the local church is key to seeing our nation transformed. As individual Christians pray for and get to know their neighbours, there will be opportunities for people to invite their neighbours to the mother-and-toddler groups, the coffee mornings, the church fairs, the parenting courses, church services and socials, and Alpha courses. As Christians get to know their neighbours, the needs of the community will become ever clearer.

Church leaders, hopefully, will also provide much-needed advice and support as the members of their congregation reach out to neighbours. It cannot be stressed enough that the key to seeing fruit from prayer and action in our neighbourhoods is a strong local church.

Prayer

We have provided prayer guides in this resource that we are happy for churches to photocopy for their congregations. If you have any similar prayer resources, we would be happy to publish these on our website as a resource for other churches.

Church co-ordinators

As a suggestion only, it may be helpful for churches to have a prayer co-ordinator. This co-ordinator asks people in the congregation to sign up to pray for their own street and feeds back to us which streets are being prayed for, as well as supplying testimonies of transformation as they start to be seen. We hope to become a place where people can find "God News stories." If, as a church leader, you would like your church to partner, please contact us. Alternatively, if you have your church leader's permission (Neighbourhood Prayer Network will check with your leader), please contact us if you want to be a church co-ordinator.

Care and share

Please see suggestions in the Diary of the Year on page 224.

A group of churches working together in a postcode
(Please note: this also works for Adopt a Street, Pray for Scotland, Love Your Street(s))

Postcode co-ordinators
We are hoping that each postcode area of the UK will have a postcode co-ordinator.

Role and responsibilities
The aim of a postcode co-ordinator is to work with churches and church leaders to map out the postcode area and to try to ensure that every street has a Christian praying for that street.

- To begin with, it is helpful to find out where people in your own church live and if they are willing to register that they are praying for their street.
- Later, co-ordinate with other churches to ask them to register where people are praying.
- Look at a map and see if there are areas that are not covered in prayer and target them with prayer walks.
- If churches are working closely together and church leaders are in agreement, encourage prayer triplets to form with members from other churches based on geographical location.
- Feed back good news stories.
- At a later date, once or twice a year organise a prayer meeting across churches in your area to pray for your locality.

Please contact us if you feel you would like to become a postcode co-ordinator at admin@neighbourhoodprayer.net.

www.neighbourhoodprayer.net

"And you shall love the LORD your God with all your heart, with all your soul, with all your mind, and with all your strength." This is the first commandment. And the second, like it, is this: "You shall love your neighbor as yourself." There is no other commandment greater than these.

Mark 12:30–31

Unity

THE IMPORTANCE OF UNITY IN THE CHRISTIAN CHURCH

by Rev. Les Isaacs OBE, CEO.

Jesus said,

> *A new command I give you: Love one another. As I have loved you, so you must love one another. By this all men will know that you are my disciples, if you love one another.*
>
> (John 13:34–35 NIV 1984)

The church is one Body; it preaches one hope; it lives by one faith; it loves one Lord. We need a greater sense of this unity, the "oneness" that Jesus talked about, if the church is going to have any lasting impact on our society in the twenty-first century. Not only do we have to have the same attitude as Jesus (loving one another), but we also have to be intentional in terms of pursuing this unity with our brothers and sisters in Christ.

An officer of the former commissioner of the Metropolitan Police once asked me if I could help "get the churches together." This, he told me, was one of the commissioner's aspirations. I remember my response to that officer as he shared with me the commissioner's vision for church unity. I said that the commissioner's aspiration was rather ambitious. I told him Jesus had been trying to bring the churches together for the past 2,000 years... and He was still working on it!

We need two things if we are going to see unity among churches and denominations. First, we need to be a praying church. Second, we need to be a church that seeks to turn those prayers into a reality. The challenges we face in our time are too vast for any one person or congregation or denomination. We need a collaborative approach. Unity is strength.

I give God thanks for the thousands of church leaders who are pursuing unity within their local community. I would encourage us, as we pray for unity, to go to fellow Christians who have a different theological point of view and seek to be reconciled with them, so that our Lord Jesus will be glorified.

I believe this is possible. I believe this because I know that up and down the country, and in other countries, thousands of Christians have united to work together to serve their community as street pastors and school pastors. I encourage us all to build on this and to hold to Jesus' teaching of love and oneness.

UNITY, THE ORDER OF ST LEONARD AND OUR NEIGHBOURS by Bishop David Carr (OSL).

"Who are my neighbours?" I hear you say.

That has been the question asked since Jesus commanded us to love them! To love is an act of the will, not of the emotions. Unity is also a deliberate action implemented after due thought and searching. To love or to be in unity says as much about us as it does about the ones we seek to love.

When you love people, it is not on the basis of a reciprocal act. The Lord loved me while I was still alienated from knowing that love. He loves me no less now that I have fully embraced that love; I just appreciate Him more.

We are creatures of culture and easily implant our pleasures or prejudices on people or even other denominational Christians.

When we love others, we can dwell in unity, not based on agreement on all aspects of life and its philosophies or doctrines, but on the essentials that become the stepping stones to faith.

The great objection to unity is the dogmatic approach taken by all Christian groups over the "interpretations of belief" rather than the "agreement of belief."

These issues confronted me over ten years ago, when I was pastoring what is commonly called a "mega" church; I realised that two main issues remained unresolved in my life. Where did the practical aspects of ministry fit into my theology, and what about those groups of Christians who, being of a traditional nature, found no resonance in me?

Matthew 25

The Lord soon chose to speak to me through Matthew 25:31–46. This scripture brought me to tears: "If you do not do this to the poor, you are but a goat!" (verse 45, paraphrased).

From this challenge, we started "Helping Hands", each person from our church bringing one tin of food each week. This has now grown to sixteen churches of differing denominations and twenty-three schools coming into unity to feed the poor of our community, working with social services and the probation service. Over time, the project grew into furniture stores, school clothing, working with autistic children, caring for those with grief, financial, marriage, divorce and recovery problems, and the realisation of the needs of those with cognitive difficulties. In this very action the disenfranchised have been ministered to and Christians spanning many denominations have come together for a purpose.

Do people come to church because of this philosophy? Yes, yet that is not the driving force. We are called to live and preach the Kingdom; out of that the Lord builds His own church.

Genesis 26

It was this second scripture that also changed my whole concept of the Kingdom. Isaac wished to reopen the wells of his father that had fallen into disrepair, yet with the mandate that they retained their original names. It is estimated there are over 33,000 Christian denominations and groupings in the world today! If this lack of unity and oneness is seen by the Lord, what must the world think? Out of this scripture, I was called to move from my denomination, which was a very sound and effective group of churches that I had served, to a historic group that had been conceived in a Wesleyan revival, yet had now lost the reality of the fire of God.

In January 2002, the Order of St Leonard formed, a lifestyle that enables the four streams of Christianity to fellowship without leaving their preferred covering, be it evangelical, charismatic, liturgical or sacramental. The ability for "brethren to dwell together in unity" (Psalm 133:1) has started.

In the UK, leaders from many backgrounds are linking through a genuine Kingdom mentality. Kenya, with many differing groups and tribes, started a "Community of St Leonard" in March 2012, attracting 5,000 churches and leaders representing 1.7 million people. Rwanda, Congo, Uganda, Burundi are also joining in 2012.

Since beginning this journey of unity with the disadvantaged, we have found favour with God and man, being designated the fourth emergency service in our town, by the mayor. Our relationships with other Christians and leaders have increased beyond expectation.

In March 2012, we welcomed Bulgaria into the Order, with dialogue taking place between the evangelicals, Pentecostals, Roman Catholics and the Orthodox churches to provide the opportunity for a feeding programme. There is also opportunity emerging for some prayer and praise between the traditions.

God honours the unity and oneness of His people. Since praying over 24,000 homes in our town and issuing our own newspaper, the church has grown by 100 people in three weeks!

Neighbourhood prayer? Yes, please!

Neighbourhood care? Yes, please!

Neighbourhood unity among churches? Yes, please!

Remember, "Whatever He says to you, do it" (John 2:5).

THE **sal†box** EST. 1983
CHRISTIAN CENTRE

SALTBOX, STOKE-ON-TRENT
by Lloyd Cooke

In 2001, a secular study looking at various socio-economic indicators across England and Wales placed Stoke-on-Trent in the unenviable position as "the worst place to live in the country." This became a catalyst for Christian leaders from across denominations to meet to pray for the area.

In a spirit of humility and quiet desperation, the leaders asked God for His divine intervention. They arranged a city prayer gathering based on 2 Chronicles 7:14 NIV:

If my people, who are called by my name, will humble themselves and pray and seek my face and turn from their wicked ways, then I will hear from heaven, and I will forgive their sin and will heal their land.

Two hundred Christians gathered to cry out for God's mercy. Such was the impact of the event that similar united prayer gatherings took place once a month under the banner "IF 2C7." These evening meetings were then supplemented by monthly half-days of prayer and fellowship for leaders, and specific weeks and months of 24/7 prayer involving numerous churches in North Staffordshire.

For the next few years, the 2C7 meetings provided a deeply significant platform for greater unity across the Body of Christ. The networking of Christian leaders also became a foundation from which large city-wide evangelistic healing missions were co-ordinated and a number of mercy ministries developed. Christian leaders were encouraged to think "city" rather than just "congregation."

In 2006 a Faith Audit detailed hundreds of faith-based projects that were helping various groups within the community. The vast majority of these projects were Christian. Christian leaders became increasingly aware of growing interest in faith-based projects from secular leaders and those outside the Church.

In 2012, leaders continue to meet under the banner of "Connect." There is a growing conviction that God wants to yoke the Old Testament "if" from 2 Chronicles 7:14 with the New Testament "if" from John 11:40 NIV:

If you believe, you will see the glory of God.

There is a growing belief that community transformation will only come about after there has been a foundation of passionate united prayer allied to real community engagement and connectivity. Many Christians believe that the increasing numbers of green shoots are pointing to a new day that is beginning to dawn across Stoke-on-Trent.

SIMILAR PROJECTS

INTRODUCTION
by Rebekah Brettle

Neighbourhood Prayer Network is working closely with similar initiatives. Adopt a Street is close to my heart and is led by Wendy Thomas, who is also the national prayer co-ordinator of Street Pastors. Wendy and I have become close friends over the last few months. Adopt a Street relies on praying blessing over streets and has already led to remarkable transformation.

Following this article is a story from Ffald-y-Brenin, which also tells the story of the power of praying blessing. Neighbourhood Prayer Network wholeheartedly supports this vision and is working in unity with Adopt a Street, believing that together we can accomplish much more than we could alone.

Sporting Marvels is aiming to have 33,000 houses prayed for in the Rhondda valley in Wales (see the article on page 68).

We have come across "Lighthouses of Prayer" all over the nation: in Scotland, Norwich, Essex. Jane Holloway many years ago wrote a resource called "Community Prayer Cells: How to Be Good News Neighbours," which she has given permission for us to put on our website, www.neighbourhoodprayer.net.

This is an excellent resource and we strongly recommend it. It provides much more detail about setting up neighbourhood prayer groups and we see no need to duplicate this great resource.

Laurence Singlehurst has carried a vision for neighbours for many years and is now working with Pastor Tunde Balogun to see "Love Your Street" spread. "Love Your Streets," an initiative of Christian Nightlife Initiatives, launched in Halifax, is merging with Love Your Street.

Prayer for Scotland has been seeing Lighthouses of Prayer based on a prayer/care/share model for many years. I was shocked to discover this, as this was the model I felt God had asked me to use for Neighbourhood Prayer Network. This encouraged me a great deal. We are asking everyone living in Scotland who wants to pray for neighbours to contact Pray for Scotland (www.prayforscotland.org.uk).

The Eden Project, a ministry of The Message, is slightly different in that it encourages Christians to move into deprived areas to become salt and light in that community.

The fact that there are so many similar initiatives, not just in this country but around the world, excites me, as it means God is speaking to many people about the same vision.

Neighbourhood Prayer Network is working hard with all these agencies, to ensure that we work together rather than compete. If there are any similar initiatives that I am not aware of, please contact us so that we can also work together. Together, I believe we can see every street in the UK covered with people praying for, caring for and sharing God's love with their neighbours.

ADOPT A STREET / STREET PASTORS
by Wendy Thomas

An initiative of Ed Silvoso, called "Adopt a Street," is a project that is being used around the world and seeing God move powerfully in transforming cities.

Adopt a Street is based on Luke 10, where Jesus tells his disciples to speak peace (*shalom*) over the city. *Shalom* means "perfect wholeness in all areas." Praying *shalom* over a person or place can only be done from a heart of love. Adopt a Street asks people to adopt a street where they live or work, and pray a blessing on it, for at least a year. The idea is that all the streets in a town become adopted and, as the atmosphere in the town alters, God moves and crime falls.

We started Adopt a Street in Southend-on-Sea in mid-April last year and we have around 200 streets adopted now. Crime figures from the police show that from April to October antisocial behaviour fell by an average of 40%. Antisocial behaviour continues to fall by an average of 40% per month and in fact in December 2011 fell by 64%.

You have a chance to join in with this by adopting a street today! My vision is to see every street in the nation adopted. Can you imagine the difference to our nation if this happened? Come on, join in and be part of it!

The streets of your town are its lifeline. When you adopt a street and use your spiritual authority to pray blessing, you are helping the people who live, work and travel on that street. You will also have an impact on bringing down crime rates, drug use, aggression, family breakdown and the general suffering of people in that street. Blessing changes the spiritual climate over the area you are praying for and ushers in the Kingdom of God.

Jesus said:

When you enter a house, first say, "Peace to this house." (Luke 10:5 NIV)

"As believers speak peace over the lost, the spiritual climate is impacted for the better, creating more opportunities for meaningful conversation and prayer." (Dr Ed Silvoso).

As an Individual
You can adopt your street online. Just visit: www.transformourworld.org/en/adopt and follow three simple steps:

1. Type in your street address, town and country.
2. Choose your own user name and password.
3. Under "Prayer Initiative choice," click on it and scroll down to "Street Pastors" under "United Kingdom."

As a Town

It is essential that Christians work together across different churches. Sign yourself up as an individual and adopt a street and then talk to groups, church ministers, etc., within your town about Adopt a Street. As a Street Pastor group, the best start is for every member of the Street Pastor group and their prayer pastors to sign up and take the initiative back to their home church to get them involved. It takes time to grow.

If you would like more information, please contact Wendy Thomas, National Prayer Co-ordinator, on prayer2@streetpastors.org.uk or visit www.transformourworld.org.

Other stories in this guide linked to praying blessing are "Ffald-y-Brenin," "Riding the Wave, Belfast," and the prayer-walking guide on page 162.

Neighbourhood Prayer Network and Adopt a Street are working in partnership.

"You will also have an impact on bringing down crime rates, drug use, aggression, family breakdown and general suffering of people in that street."

FFALD-Y-BRENIN

(This article is written with kind permission of Roy Godwin)

"Every week we speak blessings over our neighbours and immediate locality. In Luke 10 we read that Jesus taught the disciples to declare peace over a village or town before entering it."

The story of Ffald-y-Brenin, told in the book *Grace Outpouring* by Roy Godwin and Dave Roberts, has captivated the imagination of many Christians throughout the UK and beyond. Many who read the book have asked, "Is what is happening there possible where *I* live?" I will not spoil a great read (writes Rebekah), but will say that as a result of praying prayers of blessing over their local village in Pembrokeshire, Wales, the lambs have begun to have an unusually high amount of twins, a member of the occult has said that it is impossible to do any occult practices in the area, and drug dealers have stopped meeting in parts of the village. In this book we are told of people who are not Christian arriving at the door of this house of prayer, not fully understanding why they are there and being overcome with an experience of God, often going on to make a commitment to Christ. Others have experienced physical healing.

As I was reading the book, these words bounced off the page at me:

> Our vision was prompted and expanded by the Lord. If Jesus could come and be in our house, why couldn't we share the lessons we had been learning with many others and see a multiplication in the land of local houses of prayer – houses where it is rumoured that Jesus is present, with the life-giving word of God, mercy and forgiveness, healing and hope, all being poured out to their neighbours? (p. 158)

Later, Roy writes:

> A local house of prayer may be started by an individual, but as soon as possible there should be a minimum of two or three people who have a desire to identify with a particular locality – not a large one, maybe even a few streets. Fuller detail is shared on our initial training days, which are now held several times a year, but to create a house of prayer demands that we are personally becoming a house of prayer ourselves. Cleanliness is required in our inner being and in the physical house in terms of any sinful or questionable material. Both we and the house need to be Holy before the Lord. Heart attitudes need to be evaluated. There is a strong tendency for Christians to criticise and judge people and behaviours we term sinful. In a local house of prayer we are going to change all of that and have a heart to love and to

bless, to see good and trust God to deal with the bad. We are going to speak light into darkness and life to the dead, not in judgement, but in compassion and love for the sake of Jesus. (p. 161)

A Prayer for Your Street

I bless every home in the name of Jesus. I bless every wholesome enterprise, that it may be fruitful. I bless the hearts of the people in this community in the name of Jesus, that they may be softened and healed and become increasingly receptive to the voice of God. (p. 163)

Turning Prayer into Action (p. 163)

1. What is good and wholesome within this community that I could bless practically by affirmation and support with time or money? What do I see that God has sown into this community which, unbeknown to the people, carries a Kingdom value?

2. Who is God putting in front of me that I should show kindness or mercy to? Is there someone we should bless by becoming the neighbour from heaven instead of the infamous neighbour from hell? (That does not equate to becoming a well-meaning busybody who is a pain in the neck, by the way! Sensitivity is called for. It might be somebody who's been unwell and housebound. It might be someone who doesn't know where to turn next because of personal or family issues. It might be somebody who can't cope with their children or their garden.) In practical ways, is there anybody that I can show mercy to?

3. Who is God putting in front of me that I might clearly share the gospel with?

As you can see, the vision is so similar to what Neighbourhood Prayer Network is hoping to achieve. If you want to set up a local house of prayer along the lines of Ffald-y-Brenin, please visit the website www.ffald-y-brenin.org and let us know at www.neighbourhoodprayer.net to encourage us as we seek to cover the whole of the UK with Christians praying for and getting to know their neighbours. Also, please read the book!

LOVE YOUR STREETS
by Paul Blakey MBE

In February 2011 we launched, with HOPE, "Love Your Streets." This is a basic idea around community social action, trying to develop nice communities and encouraging people to do nice things for people. Examples of what we are suggesting people do are:

- Call on a neighbour when it is snowing to check they are OK.
- Help the elderly with their shopping.
- Try to be a nicer driver.
- Say "thank you" to the bus driver, to the shop keeper, etc.
- Do a Big Lunch at the annual Big Lunch in June every year.
- Do a community clean-up.
- Pray for your neighbours.
- Hold "In Bloom" competitions.

"Love Calderdale" was a big community festival taking place in a square in Halifax. Many churches were present in the town; there was free music, food and massages; and 9,000 people attended the event.

Jean Blakey writes:

> On Easter Saturday we joined with other churches in the town to distribute hot cross buns. We simply set up a table with 500 hot cross buns and serviettes on the shopping precinct and handed them out to people as they passed. Some said no, some stopped to ask why, some chatted further and some asked for prayer – a very simple act of taking love to the streets and the people of our town led to some profound conversations.

"The secular media picked up a #do1nicething on Twitter."

Love Your Street originally started in Halifax, but other areas have started to take up the initiative. A church in Middlesborough did a community clean-up last Easter, collecting a number of bags of rubbish and making the area a nicer place to live in.

The secular media picked up a #do1nicething on Twitter. Every day a suggestion was made of one nice thing you could do in your neighbourhood. While this initiative has its origins in the Christian community, they are targeting the whole population, of all faiths and none, to take part.

This project is part of Christian Nightlife Initiatives which Street Angels and Town Pastors run through. Neighbourhood Prayer Network is an official partner of this project, because it encourages people to reach out to their neighbours in practical ways. We are encouraging people at Lent to take part in the #do1nicething campaign over Lent, this year and every year. We have linked this to our "Forty Days of Prayer" guide over Lent and hope that you will consider joining in the campaign and tweeting. The tweets and dates will vary from year to year, so check out either www.neighbourhoodprayer.net or www. loveyourstreets.org.uk for the recommended daily tweet, to spread this idea across the population. See page 124 of the guide for further details.

LOVE YOUR STREET – LONDON AND BEYOND
by Pastor Tunde Balogun

Pastor Tunde Balogun

Love Your Streets and Love Your Street are in the process of merging. Pastor Tunde writes from his perspective:

Love Your Street is a secret army of Christian and most especially regular people with a mission of positively impacting on the entire geographical landscape of the United Kingdom. With as little as a sense of personal responsibility for a street where you live, work or pass through regularly, we would create a canopy of prayer and social responsibility over the entire boundary of our beloved nation.

Can you imagine what would happen if on every street in England there was one Christian who is committed, firstly, to loving people on that street unconditionally? Secondly, to have their spiritual welfare at heart, regardless of whether they ever respond to any Christian ideas. Thirdly, to build a community that serves the street by whatever creative means available.

Love Your Street is an initiative designed to cover all our streets in prayer, starting from London and stretching beyond. It is to be anchored by churches and the already existing local expression of Christians. This is important because we believe in the power of prayer and its ability to positively impact our community and everything that makes up our community. Our collective effort means that our community is covered in clouds of prayer regularly and consistently.

Why Love Your Street?

Our postmodern world has made us neglect the known virtues that have always been the contributing factors for building an authentic community of people with genuine reality of expression. The principles of sacrificial love (John 3:16) and unconditional love (2 Corinthians 5:16) are gradually fading ingredients for service, deadening how much we give of ourselves to others as Jesus did, even if it costs us.

Through Love Your Street (LYS), our prayer commitment for our adopted street will not only give God the opportunity to restore our broken society; the godly sense of spirituality will also develop and increase genuine "love thy neighbour" types of relationships, friendship and neighbourliness. These will ultimately build stronger communities and a nation we all are proud of. The beauty of this initiative is that we are not helplessly waiting and depending on our leaders to bring about better days; instead there is a collective responsibility to take our destiny into our hands and do something that matters.

Laurence Singlehurst

How To Be a Street Lover

Wouldn't it be amazing if each street of our community had someone who was committed to praying for it and making it a better place? As individuals, families, small groups, churches and Christians across villages, towns and cities we can make that a reality by adopting a street each to look after! It's a great way to start getting involved in your community and understanding its positive and negative aspects.

Anyone can put this into practice and you don't need any resources to make it happen.

- Pick a street you will commit to adopting. It could be where you live, where your small group meets, or a road you walk down regularly on your way to work, school or the shops.
- Pray for your street. You could do this every time you walk down it or set aside a specific time each week or month. Furthermore, thank God for the good things that you see there. Pray about the bad things, asking Him to bring change. Ask God what you can be doing to make a difference in that street.
- Take action. As God leads you, start to do things to bless that street and make it a better place. It could be as simple as picking up litter as you walk down it, or perhaps you will see a greater need in that area such as meeting someone who is homeless and in need of some food.
- Make friends! Greet people as you walk, start conversations, ask them about their needs and talk to God about their needs. If you ever have the opportunity, share God with them. Purposefully and prayerfully look to start relationships with people who live or work on your chosen street. Start with one person or family and commit to praying for them and blessing them in any way you can.

This idea will be best driven by individuals but could be adopted around villages, towns and cities with someone co-ordinating which streets have been adopted so that each one is covered. It would be fantastic to have regular prayer backing up the initiative, praying for situations arising in streets and keeping each Christian covered in prayer as they seek to bring God's Kingdom to their street.

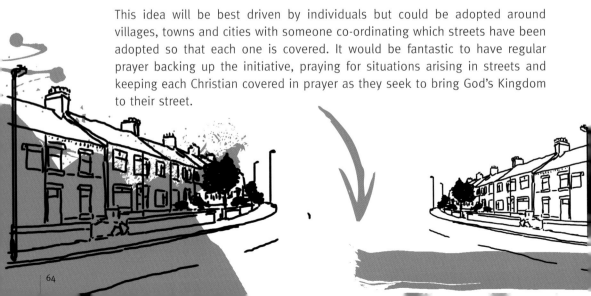

Co-ordinating Effort

- Decide which street(s) you want to pray for. You can choose the street you live on, the street your child(ren)'s school is on, or any street that you feel a burden to pray for.
- Share this idea with your church, cell group, house fellowship leader and Christian friends; and do ask for their support in this enterprise.
- We are hoping people will commit to pray for their specific street for a long period, but you can always choose to pray for a shorter period.

Let us know how it's going! Send an email with updates, insights, prayer requests and praise reports.

Need Some Ideas?

Jane in Australia loves crafts. She dropped a note to the people in her street to say that Wednesday night was her craft night and, if anybody would like to join her, to feel free to come. She has a regular gathering every Wednesday night. In this way Jane is demonstrating her sacrificial love, and out of this and through appropriate conversations she is also demonstrating that she has the spiritual welfare of those in her street at heart.

Tom in London has two parties a year, inviting the neighbours who are close to his house. Recently, as he lives in a cul de sac, he and another neighbour organised a summer barbecue for the whole street, and most people came.

Peter in Stevenage runs the Neighbourhood Watch for his street and seeks to make sure that the homes on his street are as safe as possible. In this way he demonstrates his unconditional love.

Judith in York seeks to identify who the frail, lonely and vulnerable are in her street and is a good neighbour to them. She has made an effort to know all these people and regularly drops in to check if they are all right.

These are just some of the ideas you could use.

LIGHTHOUSES OF PRAYER – PRAY FOR SCOTLAND

Lighthouses of Prayer are groups of two or more people who agree together to pray, care and share the Good News wherever they are. This can happen in a neighbourhood or workplace, or can involve people from different churches who live in the same area. It could simply be in their street as they pray for their neighbours, reach out with acts of kindness and befriend those around them. When this praying and caring culture has been established, opportunities to share our faith are often more readily available to us. Telling people about the Good News is often easier when they have already, through our prayers for them and our care towards them, experienced something of what it means.

There are over 100 towns and cities around the nation in which Lighthouse groups are now meeting. This vision is certainly impacting Scotland.

In October 2008 there was a Pray for Scotland conference in a lighthouse at Gairloch. As a result of that conference a number of Lighthouses of Prayer groups now meet together at least once a year to share what the Lord is doing in their area. It is such an encouragement to hear how the Lord is working in different parts of the nation. As we meet, we ask about and share what the Lord is saying or doing in our area. Here are some examples of what has been shared about ways to show we care.

A number of the groups have prayer-walked their towns. This has included praying and staking the high places and entrances, claiming the land and believing for 1 million souls to be saved in Scotland.

Other groups have prayer-walked new housing estates and delivered spring bulbs, chocolate bars or home baking, and even red roses on Valentine's Day.

Here is an example of a personal testimony: "Last year my neighbour who is self-employed shared that he was struggling to get work. A couple of weeks later I asked how things were going; he said he was turning work down as he was so busy. A year later he is now a sub-contractor and has a more stable income."

As we pray for our neighbours and communities, the Holy Spirit gives us opportunities to care and share and show the love of Jesus.

SPORTING MARVELS – A VISION FROM THE VALLEYS
by Phil Davies

"What would you try for God, if you knew you couldn't fail?"

This was the question posed by an Elim minister called John Bullock, pastor at Porth's Gatehouse Church, on Friday 5 July 2002. Sitting with him were three of Welsh rugby's more notorious former "bad boys" – brothers Chris and Clive Jones and their friend, Phil Davies, who had all given their hearts to the Lord in the early 1990s.

"The question really went off in Phil," John said. "He immediately downloaded a strategy to put a team of positive Christian role-models in front of the kids in the Rhondda, to change the way they think, encourage them to make wise choices, and to encourage them to stay away from the social evils so prevalent in modern-age teenage society. 'Sporting Marvels' had been birthed; its goal: to put a positive Christian role-model in front of every school-age child, every day, forever, until Jesus returns!"

Phil believed in it so much that he walked away from a six-figure salary and a high-profile role as Newport rugby's director of communications to pursue the vision full time.

"Praise God that John persevered with us," Phil said, taking up the story. "We'd been meeting for prayer and fellowship every Friday morning since 1993. John always felt that there was a bigger reason for us to meet than just our individual need and development, and he would often say that if you can transform the few, you will transform the many.

"Rhondda is a community that faces many challenges, and for teenagers especially, the pressures have never been more intense. Drugs, alcohol excess, early engagement in sexual activity, teen pregnancy, pornography, violence and criminality all contribute to the problem. Add in the more general issues of ill-health, unemployment and the facts that, according to the 2001 Census, Rhondda was both the poorest part of the UK and incredibly, for a place that was at the heart of the 1904 Great Welsh Revival, had the lowest proportion of population regularly attending church in the UK – less than .9 of 1%! We're battling to change the thinking of a generation and doing the only thing we can: standing on Luke 1:37, believing that nothing really is impossible with God.

"In October 2002, my good friend Carl Brettle showed me a leaflet for a community transformation conference in Guatemala that he thought we should attend in three weeks' time. During this conference, God gave us a monumental prayer vision for a mighty prayer-warrior army numbering 33,000. When we returned to Wales we found out that there were 33,087 homes in Rhondda!"

While in Guatemala, a gently spoken Korean pastor called Ariel Kim spoke over Phil and Carl: *"The Lord says that... Europe needs a revival... I will use Rhondda to be the example in the area of transformation of community, revival and even reformation. Rhondda will not be one of the examples; it will be THE example, and many examples will follow what I do in Rhondda."*

The prayer vision and the rest of the Guatemala adventure changed the entire context for Sporting Marvels and ushered in a vision for wholesale community transformation at a level that could speak to, encourage and inspire others to do likewise.

Against all the odds, Sporting Marvels started on time, in September 2003. The seed has gone forth every day since, while the prayer vision, renamed "Delta Force" in 2005, now numbers over 15,000 prayer warriors from forty-seven different countries, the vast majority East African. There are even five Delta Force national prayer co-ordinators: one in each of Malawi, Rwanda, Burundi, Uganda, and Tanzania.

"The 33,000 prayer-warrior army is for more than just Sporting Marvels," Phil said. "It's the engine, the energy, for God's plan to bring Rhondda to a place of wholesale community transformation – and for anything that falls under that umbrella – so that the Rhondda can affect, bless and encourage communities all over the world to do the same.

"Our Marvels are quality role-models, kid magnets, who are great adverts for the Kingdom. They have the platform, access, influence and, above all else, the heart and passion to really make a difference. Many of them were kids we've been working with for years; guys who've made the quantum leap from influenced to influencers! Working full time in the comprehensive schools and one afternoon a week in the primary schools, the Marvels are character coaches teaching values like commitment, respect, integrity, perseverance and self-discipline, all within a Biblical context with everything pointing to the Lord.

It's a remarkable story, one that's cost over £2 million to reach this point. But the Sporting Marvels magazine, *Spotlight*, is full of feedback from head teachers and children – all saying, in effect, that the seed goes forth and does not return void."

"We want Sporting Marvels operating full-on in every comp and in every primary school of Rhondda. That's going to take another nine or ten workers and an annual budget of £500,000. We need 18,000 more prayer partners to sign up for the prayer-warrior army. At present, we're asking prayer partners to sign up to pray for one of Rhondda's thirty-four villages, but the goal is to move to street level by 2014, and beyond that to house level."

For more information, including how to sign up as a prayer and/or financial partner, please visit www.sportingmarvels.com or call 01443 434281.

THE EDEN NETWORK – WHAT IS IT? by Matt Wilson

A Focus on Urban Communities

What fills your mind when you hear the phrase "inner city" or "council estate"?

Rows of terraced housing? Forbidding concrete tower-blocks? Layer after layer of graffiti? Menacing gangs peering out from under their hoods? Or how about an old fella wobbling on a ladder to water his hanging basket? Or a group of mums chatting over their buggies while their kids play in the park? Or a dad splashing his son as they wash the car together? Of course the reality could be all these things at the same time. Eden is a network of Christians who have recognised this and have been willing to enter the contradiction and challenge of life in our nation's most deprived urban neighbourhoods,

Eden is an initiative of The Message Trust which has been communicating the love of Jesus to teenagers for twenty years. During the mid-1990s The Message Trust's evangelistic band, called The Tribe, were making contact with thousands of

completely unchurched teenagers in deprived parts of Manchester, and many were having genuine encounters with God. However, getting them to connect with a local church in order to grow in their new-found faith was a different matter.

A profound change was needed – not simply a new type of programme in the church, but a new type of presence of the church, right in the heart of the community.

Strategic meetings were held with forward-thinking church leaders, and all agreed there was a need for a fresh approach toward these young people who were so obviously alienated by church culture. As a result, in 1997, the first Eden team was formed. Its aim was to see young people, and the forsaken communities in which they lived, transformed by the power of God. The method used was inspired by St John's description of Christ's arrival into the drama of history:

> The Word became flesh and blood, and moved into the neighborhood.
> (John 1:14 MSG)

Once the first pioneering Eden team was formed and began to make an impact, many more followed. Fifteen years on, hundreds of people have followed their example and become "downwardly mobile." Together they have written Eden's living story with their passion and perseverance. Their impact has been tremendous: the lives of literally thousands of young people have been touched and changed in the darkest corners of some of Britain's most challenging cities.

A TEAM EFFORT

In the New Testament, especially in the book of Acts, we get a glimpse of the way the early church grew rapidly. Always in the thick of the action were the apostle Paul and his friends. It's from Paul that we get the concept of "tent-makers" – people who have a skill or career that enables them to be financially secure while offering free time to community ministry. This is the way that most of the people on Eden teams around the country choose to live.

Sandra's story

"I've been part of the Eden team in Hattersley, a poor council estate on the edge of Manchester, for eight years. During that time I've been working full time as an IT manager and giving my spare time as a volunteer. I live here with my husband Simon and it's great to be able to share ministry with him, the rest of the team and the church that we have planted."

Amongst the teams there are GPs, teachers, midwives, students, factory workers, entrepreneurs, accountants, administrators, hotel managers, nursery nurses, checkout girls, teachers, council officers... pretty much everyone you could think of really. By creatively pooling their spare time and their talents, they can facilitate a huge number of activities in order to bless hundreds of young people and families in the communities they have chosen to adopt as home.

Each Eden team has a full-time team leader who oversees the activity and provides direction for the team; ultimately though, Eden is nothing without its committed tent-making volunteers. An optimum team size is around a dozen people all living locally as salt and light in the same inner-city area. With a servant heart, reflected in an attitude of being prepared to get stuck in and getting their hands dirty, they serve God through serving their community in numerous ways, great and small. They have all:

- responded to the call of God on their lives: their first commitment is to Christ, to know Him and to make Him known.
- committed to living long term (typically a minimum of five years) as salt and light in the target community.
- become part of the local partner church and are actively involved in its life.

Eden team members may be single young adults, married couples, families or more mature people seeking a deliberately different lifestyle.

Family of peace by Susie McGibbon

It was one of the first youth drop-ins and we were all raring to go, expecting God to do stuff but not sure what would come up. As we were still only just getting to know many of the young people, we set aside a two-minute slot at the end of the night to share a bit about ourselves, to let them know we were Christians and to talk a little bit about Jesus.

At the end a teenage lad approached my husband Rob and said quite matter-of-factly, "Do you know anything about ghosts?" There was a bit of a hush as the rest of the team all turned their ears to hear Rob's response. "Not a lot," he said, "but I know God is bigger than ghosts." The lad went on to explain that he and his friends had been freaked out that week by the ghost in his house, and that his mum hadn't slept for years because of it. Rob offered to come over to the house with me, to pray with this lad and his mum. I remember having a complete mix of emotions such as, "Gee thanks, Rob, for volunteering me" and "Come on, God, You'd better do something here or we'll look really stupid," and also "I hope his mum lets us through the front door!"

We went to the house immediately, with a few of the other teenage lads trailing behind at a short distance, curious about what was going to happen. His mum answered the door saying, "What's he done?" We explained that her son wasn't in trouble. She was moved to tears when we explained why we'd come, and she invited us in. Her son and a few of his mates came in too as spectators.

Inside she talked about how she was scared, exhausted and desperate but didn't think anyone would ever believe her. She was overwhelmed that we believed her and wanted to pray with her. We didn't do any freaky praying and casting out; we just prayed gently that Jesus would reign and that His Spirit would live in the house. She was so grateful, and amazingly even the teenage lads sat and prayed along with us.

Later in the week we asked her how she was doing and she said she had slept well every night and felt peaceful! Since that time, God has been working in a really special way in that family. They have become what you might call a "family of peace" for us, and through them we've got to know lots of other people.

What Eden Teams Do

- Live missionally, long term, in a disadvantaged community
- Use their spare time to befriend young people and families in that community, sharing life and the love of Christ with them
- Give at least five hours per week to organised community activities with a priority towards youth, examples being: detached street work, mentoring schemes, sports activities, performing arts groups, homework clubs, mums-and-tots activities, home-based dicipleship groups, etc.
- Help to resource and grow the local church in that community

What Churches Who Like The Sound of Eden Need to Know

- There are two ways to relate to the Eden Network: firstly, a closely involved working relationship, which we call Partnership; secondly, a looser relational involvement, which we call Association.
- The Partnership option is exclusively available to churches ministering in communities located in the worst 10% of neighbourhoods according to the Indices of Multiple Deprivation. Partnerships also only operate in regions where Eden has a "Regional Hub" – which are currently located in Merseyside, Greater Manchester, Yorkshire, the North East, Humberside and Greater London.
- The Associate option is offered to any church or Christian group, anywhere in the country, that desires to make a difference in a disadvantaged community. Eden offers all sorts of resources, tailored to suit local needs and priorities.

Small house, big dreams by Jenny Brown

I grew up in a small house in Salford with my mum, dad and seven siblings. Where we lived was one of those places where people never wanted to park their car. Drug and gun crimes were not uncommon. None of my family were Christians – my sister and I went to church at Christmas and Easter but that was it.

On 30 October 1999, at the age of twelve, I attended a concert which followed a week where The Tribe had led all the RE lessons in my school. Towards the end of the evening, Deronda from The Tribe sang a song and we were all asked to listen to the words and watch a video showing the crucifixion. After the song we were asked if we wanted to become a Christian. To be honest, I didn't really understand what I was signing up for, but I knew that I needed God and He would help me if I went and prayed that prayer.

Afterwards I got chatting to one of the Eden team who helped me understand what I'd done and invited me to their church the next day. So that Sunday I went along. The same lady was waiting for me, and after a little while the church became my spiritual home.

Soon after that, the LifeCentre opened – a local youth café run by the Eden team. I took part in all the activities: I remember twenty-four-hour prayer sessions in the loft, as well as learning how to be a DJ and how to touch-type, but my favourite activity was always arts and crafts. In December 2001, after lots of love, encouragement and support, I felt ready to take the plunge and be baptised.

In the years that followed, I became a volunteer on the Eden Bus which I used to go on as a younger teenager. I also began volunteering at The Message's major events in the summer. It was great to be involved, to be useful and part of a team. Most of all though, I wanted to be become a nurse, so I enrolled at college. After a lot of hard work I completed my vocational training and started full time on the wards. That was a few years ago now and my career's going really well. I now work in Manchester's biggest children's hospital where my current specialities are neurosurgery, neurology, spinal, orthopaedics and trauma.

Find out more about the Eden Network at www.eden-network.org.

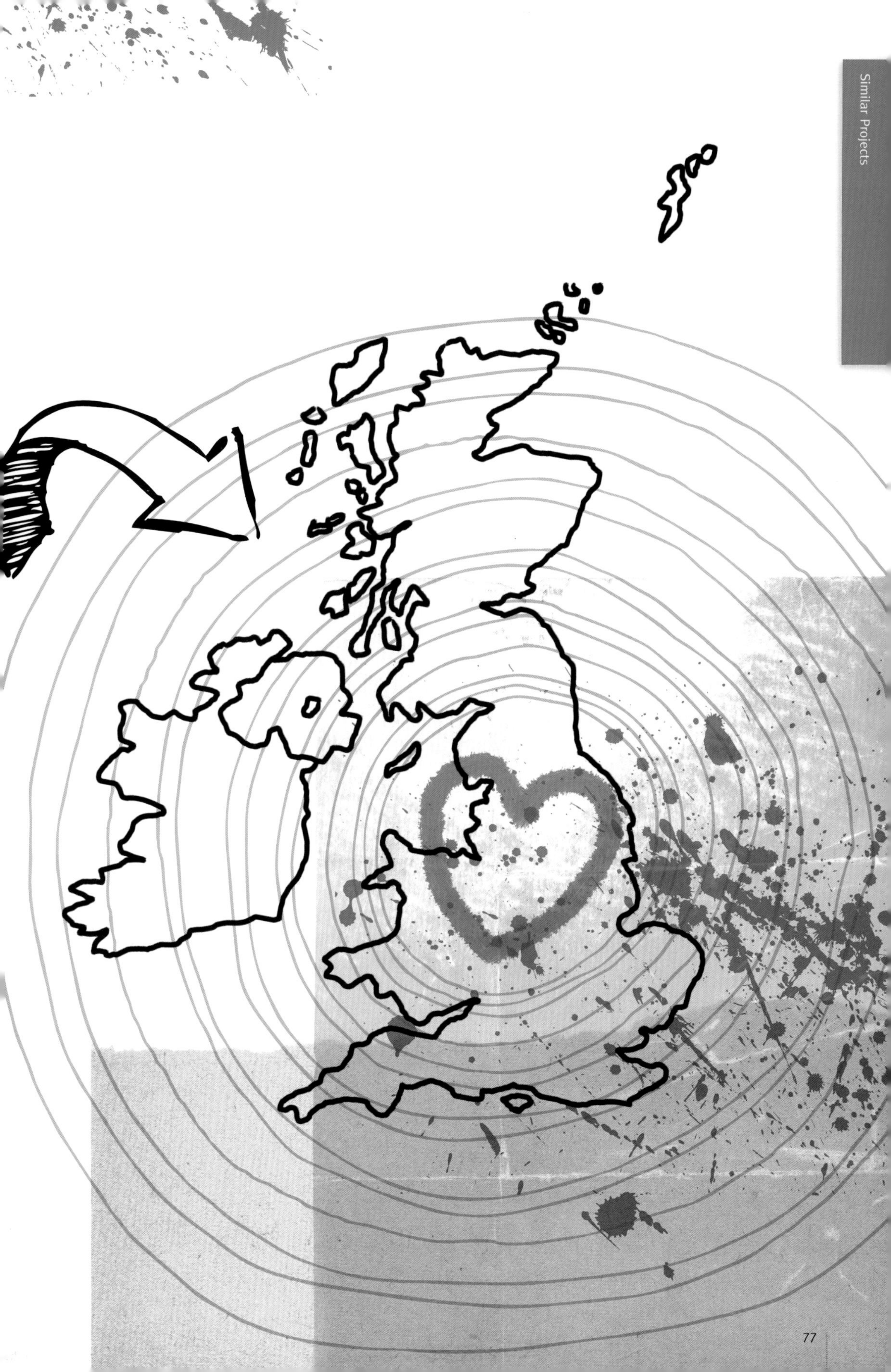

TESTIMONIES OF CHURCHES IMPACTING LOCAL STREETS

ADOPT A STREET: METRO CHRISTIAN CENTRE, BURY (FORMERLY BETHESDA PENTECOSTAL CHURCH)

This article is based on an interview with Pastor Schofield.

The congregation of sixty started this project as part of HOPE 08.

They held a meeting to which local agencies, the police and the council were invited, highlighting projects locally. As part of that meeting, over 600 people attended. A stand called "Adopt a Street" invited people to vote for a local street to be adopted. They were told that the street would be cleaned once a week and the people living there would be looked after. The street with the highest votes was adopted. What should initially have been a six-month project is still going.

The council provided equipment to clean the streets. There are currently three streets adopted with the hope of adopting another street in the next year. Two teams – one on a Tuesday evening, one on a Wednesday evening – work alternate weeks for half an hour, ensuring the streets are cleaned weekly. They wear hi-viz vests with "Adopt a Street" on the back. They pray as they clean, and speak to people passing by.

Once a week two volunteers spend an afternoon a week (three hours) visiting homes on the adopted streets. At the beginning of the project they told the residents what was happening and explained that they could say "No" if they didn't want to be visited. Three households declined, but over time they opted back into the project. On any week, not every house is visited.

Occasionally one home visit will take up to two hours, but the volunteers will not extend the visiting hours and this may be key to the longevity of the project.

Over time, as people have come to trust the church, the volunteers have been able to pray for people on the streets, help take them to doctor's appointments, do shopping when people are unwell, etc.

When the project first started, many people did not know that the church was even open; now everyone in the local community knows about it. The church has developed an excellent relationship with the local neighbourhood policing team, and people often come and tell the church leaders of suspicious things that are going on, the church then passing this on to the police. There was a situation recently where there might have been human trafficking taking place and the police were alerted to this. At Christmas the church members give out Christmas presents to the residents of all the houses.

The church has grown to 160 people over the last four years, many of whom are not directly related to the programme. However, some are. One lady was visiting her son on one of the adopted streets when he received a Christmas present. She asked why he was receiving a present from the church and decided to visit the church, becoming a Christian during that visit. Many young people from the local population attend youth groups.

Pastor Schofield is keen to point out that the church is doing this programme to show love to people and doesn't have an agenda of increasing the size of the church. They are aiming rather to bring a sense of community back to the area that was lost a long time ago.

While they have a relationship with many of the children living locally, the volunteers never enter a house when a child is home alone; a parent or adult is always there. Barbecues are held in the church car park during the year and neighbours are invited.

The church, through its regular church meeting, prays for the streets and the families they know through this project.

High points have been getting involved with the community and being able to see a positive change in people's lives. A low point occurred six months into the programme when the church congregation seemed to lose interest. At this time the pastor felt he was doing all the work, but he just kept persevering. After time, there was renewed interest and more streets have been adopted.

The idea has already spread to another church down the road who are about to adopt their first street. A school also sends out a team to clean some local streets as well.

It is difficult to quantify the impact of this initiative as it has served as an opportunity for local people to gather together, to get to know one another. The police are more aware of what is going on, and this must have a direct bearing on crime prevention. While the numbers of people living on the streets adopted and attending church are low, people see the church positively and some have become Christian, or at least are less opposed to the Christian faith. Church growth has risen 266% in the last four years, bucking the trend elsewhere. While Pastor Schofield is keen to point out that this is not directly related to the programme, he does say God is blessing the church.

Pastor Schofield feels that allowing the local community to choose the street was essential, as this opened more doors to the church. This church already had established programmes such as parent-toddler groups, fathers' groups, youth groups. Many who don't attend the church on Sunday do come to these groups.

It is my belief (writes Rebekah) that prayer, combined with genuine love and concern for others, is at the root of this growth. Perhaps more difficult to measure is the positive impact of a sense of community that is returning. I am certain that if this church was to disappear tomorrow, everyone in the local area would immediately know. Are all churches able to say this?

We encourage you to consider using this model in combination with our prayer resources to impact your local streets.

Please note: this project is not related to Adopt a Street / Street Pastors.

REAL NEWS, SOLIHULL
by Mandy Cooper

Newspapers Delivered to 24,000 Homes and a Blessing Prayed over 80,000 People

In February 2011 Pastor Peter Jenkins was preaching at our church. He announced, "We are going to deliver an invitation to our Easter service to every home in Solihull and reach 80,000 people."

This was news to me! As the church's designer I'd been asked to make a leaflet for the neighbours, not develop a communication tool to reach the entire region! However, over the next few days, I created a newspaper.

The cover was designed not to "reveal" that this paper came from a church. It led with a contemporary Easter story and contained "advert" style inclusions for ministries. There was also a sports section and advertising space, and inside were details of the services and church information.

To deliver the copies, we needed a plan of almost military precision. I looked at the local council websites, which listed all the properties. I divided streets into wards and counted how many houses were on each street. I grouped roads together, connected geographically, creating 300 delivery routes with around 100 houses each. I printed maps for each delivery route, listing roads and highlighting a particular number of houses. All of this took a week.

I made an appointment to see the church leadership armed with the proof of the newspaper, the maps and the plan, and presented the idea as a project. The leaders were delighted, but counselled caution, explaining that we might only get ten delivery volunteers out of a church of 2,000 people. They agreed to print all the papers – but only if I got the 300 delivery volunteers first. Pastor Dave dug out a contemporary Easter story he had written twenty years earlier, which became the headline story. Within two weeks we had 300 volunteers, all committed to delivering the newspapers and praying a blessing over every home. Using advertising revenue, the whole project cost the church just £280.

At Easter 2011, the church reported record numbers in attendance. We repeated the project at Christmas and again for Easter 2012. Our senior pastor, Dr David Carr, has reported a significant increase in attendance since Easter – and people continue to attend. In addition, people have started to visit the church's coffee shop and family centre, all mentioning the newspaper and wanting to find out more.

Looking back on it all, it only serves to prove to me that, with God, anything is possible. When He inspired this project, I had only been a Christian for six weeks!

And one last thing to close; some time later, I decided to "revisit" that very first service during which Pastor Peter had first made his comments about delivering to 80,000 people. I got hold of the DVD and watched it from start to finish... twice.

He remembers saying it; I remember hearing it. But it isn't there.

If you'd like to find out more or learn how to carry out this project for your church, visit www.neighbourhoodprayer.net for further details.

MISSIONAL COMMUNITY, IPSWICH

by Joanne Holmes

Sidegate Family Community is a recent missional community sent out by Burlington Baptist Church in Ipswich. Our vision is to share with our local friends and neighbours how Jesus makes a difference in family life. We were inspired and encouraged by the work at Ffald-y-Brenin, particularly by praying God's blessing over every good thing that is in our small network of streets. Prayer is an integral part of our community life and already we have seen God honour these prayers. For example, at Easter time we organised a family quiz in the local park with the option of returning to one of our houses for coffee and cake afterwards. We put in the structure and prayed for God to sort out the details and do His stuff. We were amazed when a total of twenty-nine of us returned to the house, including thirteen non-believers on a cold Easter weekend. We have prayer-walked parts of our area such as the park, asking for blessing and protection. In addition we have asked for God's power to break down areas of darkness (either parts of a street or local establishments) which were revealed to us through prayer; for example, we prayer-walked around our local pub, which holds psychic evenings.

Recently we challenged ourselves to pray for five families, for five minutes a day, for five weeks. God has blessed this by opening up opportunities to speak to these families and start to build relationships; some have even asked us to pray for them! Other people are now also seeking us out for prayer and a listening ear. Before being sent out, we mostly had friendships or intentional conversations with Christians. Now we are developing a much wider range of relationships with non-Christians, including people from other faiths. By actually getting out of the church building and trying to live the life and challenges we hear about in weekly sermons, we have been led into a deeper relationship and reliance on God and have an increased sense of urgency to save the lost.

Joanne and her family

RIDING THE WAVE, BELFAST

(This story was provided by Tearfund)

Combined prayer and social action have won the affection of a community in Belfast.

"People have told me they think we are a kind church," says Canon David Brown, minister of Knocknagoney Parish Church.

Canon David Brown
Minister of Knocknagoney Parish Church

tearfund

David describes Knocknagoney as an "inner city" style neighbourhood, albeit one located on the outskirts of Belfast. Unemployment and lone parent numbers are high. The shadow of paramilitary activity loomed heavy during Northern Ireland's insurgency.

Each Friday morning, the church meets with the local Presbyterian church to pray for Knocknagoney. They close by proclaiming God's blessing on schools, teachers, pupils, hospitals, the shopping centre, workplaces, workers, and the sick, isolated and vulnerable.

This spiritual blessing is given substance by practical expressions of love and care. Each Friday night, the church hall opens its doors to up to 100 children and young people. Here they can just chat or play table tennis, snooker or computer games. They also get slices of free pizza!

Knocknagoney used to feature in the top 10% of Belfast wards suffering antisocial behaviour. Now it lies in the bottom 10%. The police acknowledge the church's impact. Any sign of trouble, their first port of call is John Beattie, the church's Community Outreach Officer, who is co-funded by Tearfund. David believes the work with young people is pivotal. "They've got a place to go now and they've grown to respect the church."

When floods struck recently, the church joined with the Presbyterian church to bring relief to elderly residents. The hall was opened for hot tea and buns. Drains were unblocked and the water levels fell.

Often the simplest acts of kindness can have an amazing effect. During icy weather, Belfast City Council offered free bags of salt to clear drives. The church collected fifty and called on vulnerable residents. David knocked on the door of one man in his mid-seventies. "He just looked at me and said, 'I'm joining your church!' I told him he didn't need to, but he insisted. He's been attending church ever since."

The church has also helped community groups organise into a larger area forum so that they can speak with a louder co-ordinated voice. In one instance, some residents asked the authorities for a grit box. They were told this wasn't possible. The residents said they were acting on behalf of the Knocknagoney Area Forum and the issue wasn't going away. The grit box was installed within an hour.

As David reflects on his church's journey in community mission, he has this advice for other churches wanting to start one: "You've got to look and listen, to find the needs of your neighbourhood, which might need an audit of some form. And behind that is prayer. Walking around the area and asking, 'Lord, what is it You want us to do here?' It's finding the awareness you need to get outside of the church. Not that you don't meet in the building or invite people in, but Jesus was often outside the walls of the synagogue."

Children and adults smile at David as he drives past. He feels enthused. "We believe that God is doing something here, but we're always looking to move things forward. We just want to ride the wave!"

BALLYMENA HOUSE OF PRAYER, NORTHERN IRELAND
(This article is based on an interview with Jonathan Leaky)

Jonathan Leaky heads up Ballymena House of Prayer in Northern Ireland, but has a strong passion to see Christians across the UK setting up "Neighbourhood Watch" in their area.

Neighbourhood Watch is a national organisation supported by the police that encourages neighbours to come together to see a reduction in crime. Jonathan set up a neighbourhood watch in his own area, as he wanted to connect with his neighbours and he found it was an excuse to hold a barbecue and break down barriers. He uses this to help him pray for his neighbours. There have been no burglaries over the past two years. He has developed a good relationship with his neighbours and with the police.

Ballymena House of Prayer has a borough-wide vision for community transformation and is connected to Prayer Forum, 24-7 Prayer Ireland, Transformation Ireland and more recently Redeeming Our Communities. Every Friday, from 6.00 to 8.00 a.m., several churches are represented as they pray over maps and prophesy over neighbourhoods and streets. Every street in the town is prayed for.

The House of Prayer encourages areas to set up Neighbourhood Watch; there are thirteen of these schemes in the area at present. While Neighbourhood Watch is not a Christian initiative, it does help people pray more strategically for their areas. As a result of the relationships formed, fifteen church leaders were invited to send someone to the police station to pray with local police officers. Five police officers were prayed for individually and a map was set up on the wall pinpointing what churches were doing in the community. All local denominations were represented, including Roman Catholics.

More recently, Redeeming Our Communities has launched and a ROC café has been set up on a poor estate. Ballymena House of Prayer continues to pray for the salvation of everyone living in their area.

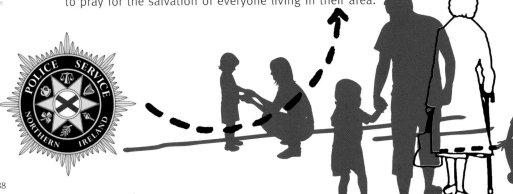

PRAYERS OF BELL FARM CHRISTIAN COMMUNITY LEAD TO DECLINE IN CRIME WAVE

The following true story is reproduced with permission from "Livability," formerly the Shaftesbury Society, and Pastor Tony Pilkington. It is based on a booklet no longer in print called "Lightening the Darkness."

Bell Farm is a West London housing estate with a population of 4,000, within easy reach of Heathrow airport. During the mid-1990s this estate saw young people begin to harass shop keepers and local residents, escalating into violence towards people and property. Young people would prevent cars driving down certain roads, jumping out in front of vehicles. They vandalised cars, set fire to them, threw bricks through houses and church building windows, and even made death threats. Bell Farm Christian Community regularly had bricks hurled through the windows during church services. The church centre was broken into once a month and, more seriously, groups were harassed when they met together.

People within the church started to pray together regularly, prayer-walking around the building. The congregation decided to organise forty days of prayer and fasting. Thirteen adults agreed to take part, two people praying each day and one on each Saturday.

In the weeks leading up to that period, the harassment and attacks against the building were as strong as ever. In the worst week, the church called the police eight times. In the middle of the forty days of prayer and fasting, the attacks against the centre subsided. In the year that followed, they only called the police twice!

Another forty days of prayer and fasting took place, this time to pray in the blessing of God. People felt a noticeable change in atmosphere. A specific answer to prayer was the appointment of a Christian police officer, who was a tremendous support. They began to pray for the police and their fight against crime.

Despite improved peace and security at the church, the underlying problems remained of intimidation of local residents. Young people continued to congregate around roundabouts and block entry or exit to the estate by throwing stones, riding bicycles slowly in the middle of the road, or even

jumping in front of cars. The church met at one of the roundabouts, taking communion together, praying, singing and pouring some communion wine on the roundabout. After this, the gang never returned and people were able to drive around the estate freely.

A small group met every evening for a week, to prayer-walk in a circle on a road where the family of the ringleader lived. Within weeks the family were evicted. On the final evening, the walkers were approached by some young people, who asked them for prayer!

Birthed in prayer, Bell Farm began social action projects for their community, today used by over 2,500 people today. See www.bfcc.org.uk.

Renewal Church, Solihull

REVILED CHURCH BECOMES THE FOURTH EMERGENCY SERVICE

In the mid-1980s, Renewal, Solihull, purchased a local primary school. Within weeks of the church moving there, the predominantly elderly population living in the surrounding bungalows began complaining to the council about the noise of cars going down their street. The council representatives were constantly turning up to investigate these complaints. The church was experiencing incredible spiritual breakthrough, yet a heaviness was felt in the building. Locals would disrupt church services, swearing at the congregation. The leadership felt there was a spiritual reason behind these attacks.

Two acts of kindness and a prayer walk were to change everything. In 1994, two members of the church, who were nurses, heard news of a lady in a nearby house who was dying; she was bedridden, obese, and doubly incontinent. They took it in turns to care for the old woman: bathing, nursing, and toileting her, and making her final few weeks a little more dignified.

At the same time, George Gardener, another church member – who was a retired gardener – decided to offer his skills to the lady who was the main antagonist, living around the corner from the church. He mowed her lawn, de-weeded her garden, and planted flowers and bushes free of charge. The woman's son, who worked for the Foreign Office, would often ring the council to complain about the church on her behalf. In the beginning she would shout abuse at George, waving a fist through the window, but eventually she invited him in for tea and they became friends. Later, just before she died, George led her to Jesus. The church performed her funeral.

As news spread of these two events, all the complaints stopped and the old people started to defend the church. In spite of this, there was still "an atmosphere" within the church building. One day the members realised that at the top of the road there was an ancient Druid burial ground named Hobs Moat. The church prayer-walked the whole area and shortly afterwards the heaviness left the building; the prayers had changed the spiritual atmosphere.

Within two years, the church had outgrown the building, moving to their current premises and laying the foundation for all their social outreach today.

Pastor David Carr says, "Prayer is the 'carpet bombing' that softens the opposition before you send in the troops. Prayer and social action combined together are a powerful and unstoppable force!"

With two simple acts of kindness and a prayer walk, a reviled church has been transformed. They provide so many services to the local community today that the mayor of Solihull has publicly declared them to be "the town's fourth emergency service."

PRAYER AND PERSONALITY
by Lyndall Bywater

Praying the Way God Made You

We human beings are each made by God; we are uniquely designed and brought to life by an endlessly innovative Creator who takes endless delight in us. One of the greatest adventures we get to go on in life is discovering exactly who we are.

If we are all made to be different, then it follows that we will do things differently. We walk differently; we talk differently; we laugh differently; and we pray differently. We are all called to prayer – that is the same for all of us, no matter what our personality – but our prayer lives will look different. How we pray will be shaped by how God made us. He knows us intimately, and He knows what kind of prayer most fits with our personality, and that is where He wants us to start.

In this section you will find the stories of five different people who pray. We don't feature them because the way they pray is perfect; we simply introduce them to you because they are all so different, and because their prayer lives reflect something of their personalities. As you read about their experiences, maybe you'll be inspired to try something new.

Connie

Prayer is my way of communicating with the unseen yet true God. What I love about prayer is that I know I am not speaking to the empty void, but that God listens and He cares. This satisfies my deepest longing for meaning and love.

I find it particularly helpful to pray with the Bible: to let Scripture raise my questions, stir up my emotions, and then let God's Word and His Spirit give me answers, or just take me nearer to Him.

I usually combine singing worship songs, Bible reading and prayer together. Singing can lead me to the presence of the Lord. I choose the theme of my songs in the following order: confessing my sin, expressing my weakness, remembering Jesus' love and His sacrifice on the cross for me, then gradually moving into songs of joy and praise. At any stage during this process, I might open my Bible and read a short passage. This can be taken from my daily Bible reading, or just be a passage that comes to my mind during worship. I pray that, as I read it aloud, God will speak to me and to my situation. I read slowly, allowing each word to sink in. Usually there will be one word or phrase that catches my eye and my mind, so I stop and pray about it.

This kind of prayer surpasses the prayer which demands help for immediate needs; it deals with the deeper needs in my soul. In this way, prayer ceases to be my "command" to make God do what I want Him to do; instead, with the Bible, prayer becomes a way for communication and communion between me and a superior yet personal God.

> David

I am charismatic. I love intercession. Liturgical ("ordered") prayer is an important part of my daily routine. But let me share my heart – the further along I travel in my journey with the Lord and the life of prayer, the more crucial and the more life-giving I find contemplative prayer.

I am far from an expert, but for me, contemplation is about quieting myself and listening to God. John the Baptist said, "He [Jesus] must increase, but I must decrease" (John 3:30), and contemplation is that idea applied to prayer.

For me, finding (well, to be truthful, *making*) a quiet time and a quiet place to turn my mind and my heart to the Lord is the key. Pondering a phrase or verse from His Word, or considering an eternal truth, or just "placing myself in His presence" unlocks the door. Listening (which in Hebrew is very connected with hearing and obeying) and not speaking; being God-centred and not me-centred; being Kingdom-focused and not worldly-minded; these are all exercises and spiritual disciplines that help me enter the holy place which is contemplative prayer.

Robin

I love to pray! I could not cope or survive without it. Am I truly so weak and dependent on it, you may ask, so utterly bereft without it? Unashamedly I say, yes, I am! Here is my experience of two forms of prayer which keep me going.

Soaking prayer

The most important form of prayer I engage in is silent or "soaking" prayer. This I need to do daily – yes, every day! I stay in stillness and quiet in my heart in God's presence, not speaking or praying out loud. Usually I will spend about

half an hour in this state. Where I can, I also put on some soaking worship music to maintain the right atmosphere and deepen my awareness of being in Father's presence. On a rare day when I can't do this, I can get withdrawal symptoms – I become quite irritable and unable to function until I can get some time away. It is as if this prayer form tunes and recalibrates my spirit.

Prayer in the Spirit (tongues)

The other type of prayer essential to keep my spirit fervent and fresh is praying in tongues. It starts off with a hunger in my soul for God, so I will usually get going by calling out loud on the Holy Spirit (sort of like priming a pump). After calling out, "HOLY SPIRIT!" a few times, worship or prayer in tongues begins to bubble up from my spirit, and this turns into a river which can go on for hours. What do I do when this is going on? I reach for the ironing board or stand behind a sink of dishes, or do other housework to help my wife. Any of these tasks tends to kick-start a flow of tongues... and I just keep going until I know I have to stop. Something usually interrupts me, or I get a nagging feeling that I need to call it a day and prepare for a meeting or take a phone call or something like that. I am usually quite sad when this happens, since while praying in tongues I get a flow of incredible peace and optimism – it's a wonderful feeling and I always look forward to it; all troubles and worries simply disappear!

Alan

For many years now I have kept a "prayer list": a list written out in a notebook with the names of all the people I want to support in prayer. For me it has been a blessed way to pray, but there came a time when my prayer list became so long that it began to feel pressurising, like an "against-the-clock" battle to fit everyone in, even when the list was divided over thirty days of the month.

I took time out before the Lord and was challenged somehow, deep within, that my prayers really ought to be rooted in the real-life circumstances of these dear people, whenever possible. So I started using the wonderful medium of email, and also little cards or notelets, to make contact with some of these individuals as they appeared on my list. What truly amazed me was that, time and time again, my note or email would arrive with a person at the precise moment when they were in desperate need, or having to make a difficult decision!

Along with this change of direction, I started to receive little "nudges" during my time of devotions, prompting me to contact people who were not on my prayer list for that day. Being a very reserved person, I fought against this nudge to contact people out of the blue. I didn't want to impose myself or create any misunderstanding through my communications. However, I try to be obedient to the Lord's promptings, so in these cases I simply send a little note or email saying that I felt led to offer a prayer for this person, using a particular phrase or scripture, and over and over again I see the ripple effect of the note being received at just the right moment.

I still retain an essential structure to my devotions, receiving prayer diaries and newsletters, and praying regularly for the persecuted church around the world, but my intercessions are now much more spontaneous, and the result is a privileged adventure and sometimes the source of more blessing than I can describe.

"...*over and over again I see the ripple effect of the note being received at just the right moment.*"

Vicki

Praying as a family is important to us, but it has not come easily in our house. With six children fairly close together in age, finding a time when we are all in the right frame of mind has been a challenge too hard for us. There have been times when it has worked really well, but then a new stage of life has come along and it has all gone "belly up"!

As some of our children have got older, they have taken more and more of the responsibility for their own relationship with God, and I have "backed off"

and allowed this to happen. They know they can ask me to pray with them, and I will and have done so, but for the most part, it has become "theirs."

With the younger three, I have found that it helps to give them something to focus on in their prayers. We get ready for school early; then we sit and read a couple of verses from the Bible, and talk about how we can pray based on what we have read. Each day is something different, and so we explore different aspects of prayer: worship, intercession, confession etc. If it doesn't happen one day, that's fine. It doesn't make us failures. It doesn't mean that we should give up. We just come back the next day and try again.

So for us, it's about grace and relationship, not duty and stress.

HOW TO PRAY THE WAY GOD MADE YOU

The exercises in this section will help you find a prayer-life which fits with who God made you to be. Remember, there is no right way to pray. You are simply spending quality time with the Father who loves you far more than you can imagine, and He is delighted to be in relationship with you. Once you've understood that, then prayer can be almost anything!

1. Finding Out Who You Are

Read these four stories about how people spent their time with Jesus:

- Luke 9:28–36 – time with Jesus suddenly gets radically exciting
- Luke 10:38–42 – time with Jesus is time to stop
- John 3:1–16 – time with Jesus is intellectual discussion
- Mark 2:1–5 – time with Jesus is putting others first and bringing them to Him for help

If Jesus were to visit you today (in human form), how would you choose to spend your time with Him? Where would you want to take Him? What experiences would you want to share with Him?

Plan out your perfect morning/afternoon/evening with Jesus. Plan about two hours with Him, being yourself, doing the things you love, connecting with Him in the way that is most natural for you. Be creative! Here are some suggestions, but these are just to get you thinking:

- Go for a long walk in the country, talking to Him as you go.
- Sit on the sofa beside Him and listen to your favourite album.
- Read the newspaper, and stop to talk with Him about each article you read.
- Make a list of the people you're feeling most concerned about at the moment, and spend a good few minutes praying for each one.
- Choose something you love (art, craft, DIY, sport) and enjoy His presence with you as you do it.

2. Finding Out Who He Is

Take some time to read these scriptures and think about what kind of God you have: Psalm 145; Luke 8; Colossians 1.

What do you need to do to make space for God to be Himself in your prayer time? How can you make sure you listen to Him as well as talk to Him? Are you open to being challenged and uncomfortable in Jesus' presence?

Choose one form of prayer you find difficult, and commit to developing it as a discipline in your life. Here are some suggestions: studying the Bible, praying for others, praise and worship, fasting, silence, meditating on Scripture, praying with other people...

3. Building a Rhythm

1. We all need to spend time in prayer every day, but the best prayer rhythms are ones which fit in with our existing daily rhythm. Where are the gaps in your day (or where could they be)? Where could you make time for prayer?
2. Prayer shouldn't be a once-a-day experience though. God's Spirit wants to walk with us through everything we do. How can you practise being aware of Him, even in your busiest moments?
3. A prayer rhythm should also include praying with others, probably about once a week. Who could you pray with?
4. Rhythms of life change as we move forward. Put a prayer rhythm together and commit to living it out for the next seven days; then review it and change it if necessary. Remember, God isn't looking for the perfect prayer rhythm; He simply wants to be your Friend and Companion on this journey of life.

NEIGHBOURHOOD PRAYER TRIPLETS

This prayer guide is intended for people wanting to set up prayer triplets to pray for their neighbours. It is particularly aimed at people who want to improve their prayer life and have not in the past attended a regular prayer group, although many others will find it helpful too.

The guide lasts for twelve weeks and assumes that people meet once a week to pray. Each week has a theme, involving some Scripture about prayer and some prayer pointers relating to your neighbourhood. We encourage you to be flexible and creative in the way you use the guide. You may wish to read out the various scriptures and written prayers, or just read them in silence and use them as a springboard for your own prayers. Let this material inspire you rather than restrict you. You may also find it helpful to keep a prayer journal to record the prayers you pray and the answers you receive.

We hope that after using this guide you will feel able to continue praying confidently in your prayer triplet, if God leads you to do so.

Note: This guide has been reviewed by many people in order to ensure that the content is acceptable across a range of denominations. At every opportunity, we have tried to let Scripture speak for itself.

Why Form a Prayer Triplet?

Throughout the Scriptures, we read of God calling His people to work together. Abraham, Isaac and Jacob travelled with their families; Moses worked with Aaron to lead the captive Israelites to freedom; the prophets worked in "companies"; King David fought alongside his troop of mighty men; and of course Jesus had twelve disciples. What's more, the imagery which the New Testament writers use to describe the church is always plural: parts of a body, soldiers in an army, members of a family, ambassadors on a mission. Jesus sent His disciples out in twos, and Paul always travelled with companions when he planted churches. Though our own individual relationship with God is vitally important, when it comes to reaching the world around us, the single-handed approach isn't enough. We need each other, and we are at our most effective when we work together.

Praying for our neighbourhoods is likely to be a long journey and, like any journey, it is better travelled together:

- Companions encourage us when we get tired and discouraged
- They help us dream bigger dreams than we might on our own
- They help us hear God more clearly
- They help us turn our prayers into actions

In prayer, we're using the authority God has given us as His children and ambassadors to bring change to our communities. Jesus said that authority should be used in groups praying in agreement:

> Again I say to you that if two of you agree on earth concerning anything that they ask, it will be done for them by My Father in heaven. For where two or three are gathered together in My name, I am there in the midst of them. (Matthew 18:19–20)

Forming a Prayer Triplet

We suggest that a prayer triplet is formed representing, where possible, three different streets. You may choose to pray with people you already know in your church, or you may want to deliberately seek out people from other churches who live nearby. We don't believe any two groups will be the same!

When you start to form a group, agree together on a regular time when you are going to meet, and how long you're going to meet for. Also discuss how you would like to pray together. It is good to decide together how the meeting should run, so that while the theme may change, the format remains the same. This will help your group grow in confidence.

In an area with a particular problem such as high crime or antisocial behaviour, two or more triplets in the same church may want to meet together to pray. These gatherings will happen less frequently than your weekly triplet meeting (perhaps once a month or once a quarter) and could take place in someone's home or in a church building.

Confidentiality, safety and safeguarding

Please keep the prayers prayed in your group confidential, except in dialogue with your church leadership. Gossip spreads fast and can be destructive to the people you want to help.

"Talk to God about broken families, step-families and children who are separated from their parents; ask for His help and healing."

Children and vulnerable adults

This guide is not suitable for children or vulnerable adults to use because of its emphasis on getting to know neighbours. While the vast majority of people living on our streets would not harm a child or vulnerable adult, we are concerned about the growing issues surrounding abuse. We would ask you to be vigilant about this risk when interacting with your neighbours.

We strongly advise that, in getting to know your neighbours, you don't put yourself in a position where you are on your own with a child, vulnerable adult or someone of the opposite sex. We also ask that all adults adhere to the safeguarding policies of your local church, and inform your church leader that you are using this guide.

Week 1: Conversations with Our Heavenly Father

> For You formed my inward parts;
> You covered me in my mother's womb.
> I will praise You, for I am fearfully and wonderfully made;
> Marvelous are Your works,
> And that my soul knows very well.
> My frame was not hidden from You,
> When I was made in secret,
> And skillfully wrought in the lowest parts of the earth.
> Your eyes saw my substance, being yet unformed.
> And in Your book they all were written,
> The days fashioned for me,
> When as yet there were none of them.
> (Psalm 139:13–16)

> Are not two sparrows sold for a copper coin? And not one of them falls to the ground apart from your Father's will. But the very hairs of your head are all numbered. Do not fear therefore; you are of more value than many sparrows. (Matthew 10:29–31)

> Jesus said to him, "I am the way, the truth, and the life. No one comes to the Father except through Me." (John 14:6)

> Yet to all who did receive him, to those who believed in his name, he gave the right to become children of God – children born not of natural descent, nor of human decision or a husband's will, but born of God. (John 1:12–13 NIV)

> For through him we both have access to the Father by one Spirit.
> (Ephesians 2:18 NIV)

Conversations with each other

In this first session of your prayer triplet, why not spend some time getting to know each other more? You could start by each telling the story of what brought you to live in the neighbourhood, and then share one thing you love about where you live and one thing you dislike.

You are of infinite value to God. He loved you so much that He sent His Son Jesus to die on a cross for you. His greatest longing was that you should "have access" to Him (Ephesians 2:18). He doesn't want you to have to pray to Him from afar, saying the right words, practising the right rituals and hoping for the best. He wants you to come right up close and talk to Him, just as you would talk to a friend.

God cares about every aspect of your life. While it is helpful to have structures for prayer, God loves to just talk with you about your day. If you didn't speak to your husband, wife, children, parents, brothers, sisters or friends, your relationship with them would not be very good. The same is true with God. If all you do is speak and listen to Him once a week at church on Sunday, then your relationship with Him will be shallow and frustrating.

Prayer is simply listening and speaking to God. God has a vast number of ways to speak: He uses Scripture, circumstances, dreams, visions, the words of other people; He sometimes puts a picture in your mind or causes a whole new idea to pop into your head; He stirs a feeling in you or causes you to see something in the world around you which reminds you of something. Never limit God by saying you can't hear Him. He can get through to you no matter who you are or how you tick. When praying together with others, often two or more people will have a similar thought. Usually, but not always, this is God speaking. Remember, God will never say anything that contradicts the Bible!

In this first prayer time, try to just speak to God as though He is physically there as a real person – as the most important Person sitting with you. Don't feel you have to use special language or complicated ideas. Just chat with Him as you have been chatting with each other.

Praying for your triplet

Spend some time thanking God for each other, and for bringing you together as a prayer triplet. Ask Him to guide you as you pray together, and to use your prayers to make a powerful difference in your community. (Remember there's no pressure to pray out loud.)

Praying for your neighbours

- Talk to God about the kind of community you'd like your neighbourhood to be.
- Talk to God about families and the struggles they face in today's world; tell Him what you'd like Him to do for families in your street.
- Talk to God about broken families, step-families and children who are separated from their parents; ask for His help and healing.
- As you think about what it means to be loved by God as a Father, ask Him to bring everyone in your street to the place of knowing that He loves them completely and unconditionally.

Everyone in the prayer triplet: Write the names down of three households each, commit to trying to get to know the people living in these houses, and commit to praying for these people by name over the next year.

Week 2: ACTS Prayer Model

In this manner, therefore, pray:

Our Father in heaven,
Hallowed be Your name.
Your kingdom come.
Your will be done
On earth as it is in heaven.
Give us this day our daily bread.
And forgive us our debts,
As we forgive our debtors.
And do not lead us into temptation,
But deliver us from the evil one.
For Yours is the kingdom and the power and the glory forever.
Amen.
(Matthew 6:9–13)

There are many models for prayer, and today's scripture shows us the one Jesus taught His disciples. You may be used to reciting the Lord's Prayer as a formal prayer, but you can also use it as a kind of template for praying, as it includes all the key elements of a prayer time (praising God, confessing our sins, asking for help etc). Another way to remember those elements is to use the word "ACTS," which stands for Adoration, Confession, Thanksgiving, Supplication (asking).

Adoration

Adoration is worship. It is taking time to stop and turn our thoughts and our hearts towards God. It is remembering and recognising what an amazing God He is. Some people like to listen to worship music, or to read out one of the Psalms. Others may want to write down what God means to them, or talk about the good things He has done for them that week. Some may not want to pray aloud whereas others will. Please do what you find most comfortable in your group.

Confession

Confession is being honest with God about the things we've done wrong, and asking for His forgiveness.

You may find it helpful to read through the Ten Commandments (Exodus 20) and silently confess before God the times that you haven't lived up to them. Alternatively you might like to base your confession on this scripture:

> Jesus answered him, "The first of all the commandments is: 'Hear, O Israel, the LORD our God, the LORD is one. And you shall love the LORD your God with all your heart, with all your soul, with all your mind, and with all your strength.' This is the first commandment. And the second, like it, is this: 'You shall love your neighbor as yourself.' There is no other commandment greater than these." (Mark 12:29–31)

Prayer:
Father God, I am truly sorry for the things I have done which have offended You or hurt those around me. I'm sorry too for the good things which I could have done, but which I chose to avoid. Please forgive me, and help me to live differently. Thank You for sending Your Son, Jesus Christ, to die on a cross, so that my sins can be forgiven and I can speak with You without any barriers. I believe and accept Jesus as Lord and Saviour in every area of my life, and reaffirm my commitment to you. Amen.

Thanksgiving

Thanksgiving is the act of remembering the good things God has done for us, and expressing our gratitude to Him. Thank God for all that you are grateful for, starting with the everyday things: a roof over your head, family, friends, food to eat, heating, running water... and anything else God has done for you, or helped you through. Remember to thank Him for the challenges as well as the blessings. Some people like to speak these prayers out, while others prefer to pray silently.

Supplication

Supplication means asking. We ask because Jesus said we should, and because our Father in heaven loves to hear our requests for help.

Using the Lord's Prayer as the template, here are some ideas of things you could pray for today. Use them as a springboard to get you started in praying for your neighbourhood.

- Father, we pray for ourselves and the things we need today. Please give us our "daily bread."
- Jesus, we pray for all our neighbours living on our streets, that they will come to know You. May Your Kingdom come and Your will be done here in our neighbourhood.
- Holy Spirit, help us to be good neighbours in our streets. Set us free from evil and help us avoid temptation. Amen.

Week 3: Forgiveness

Then Peter came to Him and said, "Lord, how often shall my brother sin against me, and I forgive him? Up to seven times?"

Jesus said to him, "I do not say to you, up to seven times, but up to seventy times seven. Therefore the kingdom of heaven is like a certain king who wanted to settle accounts with his servants. And when he had begun to settle accounts, one was brought to him who owed him ten thousand talents. But as he was not able to pay, his master commanded that he be sold, with his wife and children and all that he had, and that payment be made. The servant therefore fell down before him, saying, 'Master, have patience with me, and I will pay you all.' Then the master of that servant was moved with compassion, released him, and forgave him the debt.

"But that servant went out and found one of his fellow servants who owed him a hundred denarii; and he laid hands on him and took him by the throat, saying, 'Pay me what you owe!' So his fellow servant fell down at his feet and begged him, saying, 'Have patience with me, and I will pay you all.' And he would not, but went and threw him into prison till he should pay the debt. So when his fellow servants saw what had been done, they were very grieved, and came and told their master all that had been done. Then his master, after he had called him, said to him, 'You wicked servant! I forgave you all that debt because you begged me. Should you not also have had compassion on your fellow servant, just as I had pity on you?' And his master was angry, and delivered him to the torturers until he should pay all that was due to him.

"So My heavenly Father also will do to you if each of you, from his heart, does not forgive his brother his trespasses."
(Matthew 18:21–35)

And whenever you stand praying, if you have anything against anyone, forgive him, that your Father in heaven may also forgive you your trespasses. But if you do not forgive, neither will your Father in heaven forgive your trespasses.
(Mark 11:25–26)

When we give our lives to Jesus, we open the door to forgiveness. His death on the cross means that every sin we have ever committed or will ever commit is cancelled out – the slate wiped clean. We choose to forgive others because we have been so completely and radically forgiven by God. When we choose not to forgive others, we keep hold of something destructive, which can leave us emotionally and even physically damaged. To receive the fullness of God's forgiveness and healing in our own lives, we need to let go of past hurts, and let Him help us move forward.

It's important to remember that:

- Forgiveness is not pretending you're not hurt.
- Forgiveness is not letting people off the hook.
- Forgiveness is not saying it doesn't matter that you got hurt.
- Forgiveness is not excusing people or justifying their actions because they had a good reason for what they did.
- Forgiveness is not necessarily a one-off thing: we may need to keep forgiving the same person for the same thing for many years.
- Forgiveness is not easy, but it is possible with God.

Forgiveness is recognising that something wrong was done, feeling the pain and injustice of that wrong, but choosing to hand it over to God, so that He can be the Judge.

Forgiving others

First, ask the Holy Spirit to help you. Forgiveness is hard, and may even be impossible, without God's help. Then bring to mind each person who has hurt or wronged you. As you think about each one, choose to hand them over to God for Him to judge and put right. You may even find it helpful to visualise leaving them with Jesus at the cross.

Prayer:
Lord Jesus, I thank You that You know what being human is like, and You know what it's like to be hurt by others. Thank You that You have set me free so that I can forgive just as You forgave. As I bring to You the people who have hurt me, I acknowledge the wrong they have done and the pain I've felt, but I refuse to be held captive by those things. Today I choose to hand them over to You. You judge fairly and You know how to heal me. Jesus, heal my heart and set me free.
Amen.

Forgiving yourself

Sometimes we find it much easier to forgive others than ourselves. If that's where you are today, take some time in silence to speak to God about the things you feel you have done wrong which don't deserve forgiveness. Choose to accept that Jesus has already paid the price you're trying to pay by punishing yourself, and ask the Holy Spirit to help you forgive yourself.

Praying for forgiveness in our neighbourhoods

Prayer:
Lord, we pray for everyone living on our streets, that people will be able to forgive those who have hurt them in the past. Show them that You are a God who loves and forgives them. Give them a desire to leave their grudges behind.
We bring before You [insert the names of neighbours, or house numbers] and pray a blessing over their houses.
Help our street change in atmosphere as people let go of the past and move forward.
We especially pray for people who have been abused physically, spiritually, sexually or mentally [do not mention names]. Please heal them and enable them to stay safe from danger, now and in the future. Amen.

Prayer requests

Add any specific prayers for neighbours here, remembering to keep confidentiality.

Week 4: Love Your Neighbour!

Though I speak with the tongues of men and of angels, but have not love, I have become sounding brass or a clanging cymbal. And though I have the gift of prophecy, and understand all mysteries and all knowledge, and though I have all faith, so that I could remove mountains, but have not love, I am nothing. And though I bestow all my goods to feed the poor, and though I give my body to be burned, but have not love, it profits me nothing.

Love suffers long and is kind; love does not envy; love does not parade itself, is not puffed up; does not behave rudely, does not seek its own, is not provoked, thinks no evil; does not rejoice in iniquity, but rejoices in the truth; bears all things, believes all things, hopes all things, endures all things. (1 Corinthians 13:1–7)

You have heard that it was said, "You shall love your neighbor and hate your enemy." But I say to you, love your enemies, bless those who curse you, do good to those who hate you, and pray for those who spitefully use you and persecute you, that you may be sons of your Father in heaven; for He makes His sun rise on the evil and on the good, and sends rain on the just and on the unjust. For if you love those who love you, what reward have you? Do not even the tax collectors do the same? And if you greet your brethren only, what do you do more than others? Do not even the tax collectors do so? Therefore you shall be perfect, just as your Father in heaven is perfect. (Matthew 5:43–48)

The Bible makes it clear that love is both an attitude and an action. When we love in both those ways, something powerful is released, and neighbourhoods can totally change.

Loving attitude

- Spend time in silence and ask God to show each of you where your attitude towards people in your neighbourhood is less than loving. Ask for His forgiveness and invite the Holy Spirit to change your heart.
- Make a special commitment to pray for those you find it hardest to love. Praying for someone can be the quickest way to start loving them.
- Pray for situations in your neighbourhood where relationships are strained, where people are excluded or where people are treated with hostility (keep confidentiality).

Loving actions

- Ask God to show you how you can love your neighbours more through your actions.
  - Offering to pray for people is a sign of love. Think about giving out prayer cards in your streets, inviting people to write down anything they'd like you to pray for.
  - Is there anything God is laying on your hearts as a prayer triplet which He wants you to do for your neighbours?

Week 5: Unity and the Prayer of Agreement

I do not pray for these alone, but also for those who will believe in Me through their word; that they all may be one, as You, Father, are in Me, and I in You; that they also may be one in Us, that the world may believe that You sent Me.
(John 17:20–21)

A new commandment I give to you, that you love one another; as I have loved you, that you also love one another. By this all will know that you are My disciples, if you have love for one another.
(John 13:34–35)

How good and pleasant it is
    when brothers live together in unity!
It is like precious oil poured on the head,
    running down on the beard,
running down on Aaron's beard,
    down upon the collar of his robes.
It is as if the dew of Hermon
    were falling on Mount Zion.
For there the Lord bestows his blessing,
    even life for evermore.
(Psalm 133:1–3 NIV1984)

When the day of Pentecost came, they were all together in one place. Suddenly a sound like the blowing of a violent wind came from heaven and filled the whole house where they were sitting. They saw what seemed to be tongues of fire that separated and came to rest on each of them. All of them were filled with the Holy Spirit and began to speak in other tongues as the Spirit enabled them.
(Acts 2:1–4 NIV)

Again I say to you that if two of you agree on earth concerning anything that they ask, it will be done for them by My Father in heaven. For where two or three are gathered together in My name, I am there in the midst of them.
(Matthew 18:19–20)

Praying for unity

One of the things which confuses people most about the church is why it's in so many different pieces. Jesus prayed that we would "be one," so we join in His prayer:

Prayer for the local church:
Lord Jesus, we pray for all churches in this area, for unity in spirit and truth, within churches and between churches. Forgive us for the times when we have allowed our prejudices or preferences to divide us. Help us all to speak well of one another, and to work together for Your Kingdom. May Your people always look for the best in others, just as You did, and demonstrate Your Kingdom by loving one another. May the Christians in this area work and pray together for the good of our neighbourhood. Amen.

Could you think about holding a bigger prayer meeting for your neighbourhood, inviting Christians you know from different churches to get together?

Prayer of agreement

Jesus taught His disciples that there is power in agreement. Matthew 18:19–20 is about authority, and Jesus says that we use our God-given authority best and most effectively when we're praying in agreement. Praying in agreement involves getting together with others and tuning our hearts and our prayers to one another and to God. When what I'm praying for lines up with what you're praying for and what God wants to do, then we're all in agreement and something very powerful is released. When that agreement is between people of different churches, different generations or different races, it can have an even greater impact. God loves to hear His people praying together with one heart.

Remember though: prayers of agreement must always line up with Scripture and the values of the Kingdom; prayers of agreement should be prayers of blessing, not moaning or criticising, because God's heart is to bless our neighbourhoods with good things.

Now that you've been meeting for several weeks, is there a particular social problem or difficult situation in your neighbourhood which you all feel strongly about and which you believe God wants to change? Spend some time today praying together in agreement, asking God to bring breakthrough.

Here are some suggestions to give you an idea of what you might choose to pray about:

- high crime rates
- a family with a particular problem or crisis (be aware of confidentiality issues)
- an area nearby where there have been a lot of problems lately

Week 6: Prayer of Faith

> So Jesus answered and said to them, "Have faith in God. For assuredly, I say to you, whoever says to this mountain, 'Be removed and be cast into the sea,' and does not doubt in his heart, but believes that those things he says will be done, he will have whatever he says. Therefore I say to you, whatever things you ask when you pray, believe that you receive them, and you will have them."
> (Mark 11:22–24)

> Most assuredly, I say to you, he who believes in Me, the works that I do he will do also; and greater works than these he will do, because I go to My Father. And whatever you ask in My name, that I will do, that the Father may be glorified in the Son. If you ask anything in My name, I will do it.
> (John 14:12–14)

> But without faith it is impossible to please Him, for he who comes to God must believe that He is, and that He is a rewarder of those who diligently seek Him.
> (Hebrews 11:6)

Praying in faith is asking God for the things He has promised, and believing that He will fulfil those promises because He is faithful. Praying in faith doesn't mean we never have questions or never feel unsure; it simply means that, in spite of our questions or uncertainties, we choose to believe what God says, and trust Him to keep His word.

When praying in faith, the following things are vital:

- Check your heart first: get right with God if there's anything you need to forgive or confess.
- Check your prayers for selfish motives; the prayer of faith is about God's Kingdom rather than our own needs and wants.
- Make sure your prayers are in line with Scripture.
- When something isn't specifically mentioned in Scripture (e.g. "Should I pray for my neighbour to pass their exams?"), ask yourself whether it's in line with the sort of things Jesus valued and lived for in the Gospels. Praying in Jesus' name means praying for the things He would pray for.
- Make your prayers specific; it's harder to celebrate the answers if the requests are too vague.

Praying for impossible situations

What are the impossible situations in your street? Are crime levels high? Is there antisocial behaviour? Are you concerned about the behaviour of children, or worried about the elderly lady who never leaves the house? Do people know each other, or are they afraid to get to know each other? Does someone have an illness for which there is no cure?

List the things that you want to see change on your street, along with any prayer requests from your neighbours. Pray a prayer of faith together today to see each of these things begin to change. Don't forget to be specific!

Suggested prayer:
Lord, thank You that You hear our prayers when we come to You. Forgive us where we have chosen not to believe You in the past; forgive us where we have allowed our doubts to diminish our prayers. Thank You that You are a God who is true to Your word. Give us faith to believe that You will do what seems impossible to us.
We pray for _____, that You will _____.
Amen.

Week 7: Keep Praying

Then Jesus told his disciples a parable to show them that they should always pray and not give up. He said: "In a certain town there was a judge who neither feared God nor cared what people thought. And there was a widow in that town who kept coming to him with the plea, 'Grant me justice against my adversary.'

"For some time he refused. But finally he said to himself, 'Even though I don't fear God or care what people think, yet because this widow keeps bothering me, I will see that she gets justice, so that she won't eventually come and attack me!'"

And the Lord said, "Listen to what the unjust judge says. And will not God bring about justice for his chosen ones, who cry out to him day and night? Will he keep putting them off? I tell you, he will see that they get justice, and quickly. However, when the Son of Man comes, will he find faith on the earth?"
(Luke 18:1–8 NIV)

And pray in the Spirit on all occasions with all kinds of prayers and requests. With this in mind, be alert and always keep on praying for all the Lord's people.
(Ephesians 6:18 NIV)

You have been praying together for a while now, so make a list of the prayers you've prayed which God has already answered. Then list the prayers you are still waiting to receive answers to.

If a prayer is worth praying, it is worth praying many times. Some prayers may not be answered for several years. Have you got the stamina to keep going even when you don't get the answer you are waiting patiently for? Some people give up, not knowing how close they are to an answer. Keep going! God will reward your faithfulness and determination.

Persevering for each other

Spend some time this week praying for each other, that you will have the strength to keep going in prayer for the long haul. If you feel able to, why not share some of the things you've been praying for in your own personal life for many years, and get your prayer triplet friends to pray with you for those things today.

Persevering for your neighbourhood

When prayer takes a long time to be answered, discouragement can step in. The best way to deal with discouragement is to worship God and read His Word. As you pray for your neighbours today, punctuate your praying with plenty of worship (speaking out the goodness of God), and read plenty of scriptures out loud to encourage each other.

Week 8: Praying with Humility and without Judgment

Judge not, that you be not judged. For with what judgment you judge, you will be judged; and with the measure you use, it will be measured back to you. And why do you look at the speck in your brother's eye, but do not consider the plank in your own eye? Or how can you say to your brother, "Let me remove the speck from your eye"; and look, a plank is in your own eye? (Matthew 7:1–4)

Also He spoke this parable to some who trusted in themselves that they were righteous, and despised others: "Two men went up to the temple to pray, one a Pharisee and the other a tax collector. The Pharisee stood and prayed thus with himself, 'God, I thank You that I am not like other men – extortioners, unjust, adulterers, or even as this tax collector. I fast twice a week; I give tithes of all that I possess.' And the tax collector, standing afar off, would not so much as raise his eyes to heaven, but beat his breast, saying, 'God, be merciful to me a sinner!' I tell you, this man went down to his house justified rather than the other; for everyone who exalts himself will be humbled, and he who humbles himself will be exalted." (Luke 18:9–14)

For I say, through the grace given to me, to everyone who is among you, not to think of himself more highly than he ought to think, but to think soberly, as God has dealt to each one a measure of faith. (Romans 12:3)

Prayer for humility:

Lord, thank You that You love us completely, just as we are, and that You're at work to make us more and more like Jesus. Please help us to be humble and not to be proud, not thinking we are better than we actually are. Help us not to judge people, and forgive us where we have judged those who have lifestyles which are different from ours. Help us to show love to all people, even when we dislike things about the way they live. Help us to see people as You see them, and not to be blind to the needs they have.

Amen.

Praying for your neighbours

- Pray for people who may be struggling with addictions to alcohol, nicotine or drugs, that God will help them get free of what holds them.
- Pray for people on your street who are unemployed, sick or on benefits, that God will supply all their physical and financial needs.
- Pray for single mothers and fathers, and those who are divorced or bereaved, that God will put supportive friends and family around them.
- Pray for those living in homosexual relationships, that God will bring loving, non-judgmental friends into their lives.
- Pray for families where someone has a criminal record, that they will be treated fairly and justly.
- Pray for families affected by domestic violence or abuse, that God will rescue and heal them.
- Pray for those who may be sleeping on friends' couches because they are homeless, that they will be able to break out of the poverty cycle and find work and housing.
- Pray that all of these people will feel loved by others, have healing where it is needed, find acceptance in the local community and local churches, and come to know God as their loving Father.

Week 9: Praying for the Holy Spirit

So I say to you, ask, and it will be given to you; seek, and you will find; knock, and it will be opened to you. For everyone who asks receives, and he who seeks finds, and to him who knocks it will be opened. If a son asks for bread from any father among you, will he give him a stone? Or if he asks for a fish, will he give him a serpent instead of a fish? Or if he asks for an egg, will he offer him a scorpion? If you then, being evil, know how to give good gifts to your children, how much more will your heavenly Father give the Holy Spirit to those who ask Him! (Luke 11:9–13)

But the fruit of the Spirit is love, joy, peace, longsuffering, kindness, goodness, faithfulness, gentleness, self-control. Against such there is no law. And those who are Christ's have crucified the flesh with its passions and desires. If we live in the Spirit, let us also walk in the Spirit. (Galatians 5:22–25)

There are different kinds of gifts, but the same Spirit distributes them. There are different kinds of service, but the same Lord. There are different kinds of working, but in all of them and in everyone it is the same God at work.

Now to each one the manifestation of the Spirit is given for the common good. To one there is given through the Spirit a message of wisdom, to another a message of knowledge by means of the same Spirit, to another faith by the same Spirit, to another gifts of healing by that one Spirit, to another miraculous powers, to another prophecy, to another distinguishing between spirits, to another speaking in different kinds of tongues, and to still another the interpretation of tongues. All these are the work of one and the same Spirit, and he distributes them to each one, just as he determines.
(1 Corinthians 12:4–11 NIV)

God is looking for people who will pray for their neighbourhoods, but He's also looking for people who will go out and be the answer to their own prayers. He wants to equip us with His Holy Spirit so that we can make a difference through our day-to-day lives as well as through our prayers.

Welcoming the Holy Spirit:
Father, we thank You that You are the Giver of good gifts. Today we welcome the fresh flow of Your Holy Spirit in our lives. We put aside the things which block that flow – our sins, our fears and our hard-heartedness – and we invite You to have free rein in our lives. Father, help us to keep pushing our roots down deep in You, so that our lives produce the fruits of Your Spirit, and we become a living demonstration of Your Kingdom here in our neighbourhood.

Lord, help us to understand the gifts You have given to each one of us, so that we can use them more and more effectively. Give us boldness to use our gifts as we interact with our neighbours. We thank You that You have a purpose for all our lives; help us to walk in Your ways, so we can accomplish what You are asking us to do. Holy Spirit, we invite You to come into our lives in power so that we can be all You have called us to be.
Amen.

Sometimes our many words of prayer can get in the way of what God's Spirit wants to do or say. Pray the above prayer together; then spend ten minutes or more in silence, allowing the Holy Spirit to work in each of you. Perhaps He will speak, or perhaps He will stir a feeling or an image in your mind. Whatever He does, try not to fight Him or to make something happen – just rest in God and trust Him to work in you.

After this time, share with one another what God's Spirit was saying to you or doing in you. If you're not sure or you didn't "feel" anything, don't feel guilty! Just share what those moments of quiet were like for you.

Sometimes God communicates to a whole group by giving each person one part of a bigger picture – like a piece of a jigsaw puzzle; sometimes He communicates what He wants to say by saying the same thing to everyone. The key is to let God be God.

And if you've heard something clear from God, make sure you talk together about how you can act on what He's said.

Obey the Word of God. If you hear only and do not act, you are only fooling yourself.
(James 1:22 NLV)

Praying for neighbours

- Pray for your prayer triplet, that you will be guided more and more by God's Spirit as you pray together for your neighbours.
- Ask God's Spirit to give you specific names of people in your street whom He wants you to help this week.

Week 10: Praying in Times of Difficulty

But at midnight Paul and Silas were praying and singing hymns to God, and the prisoners were listening to them. Suddenly there was a great earthquake, so that the foundations of the prison were shaken; and immediately all the doors were opened and everyone's chains were loosed. And the keeper of the prison, awaking from sleep and seeing the prison doors open, supposing the prisoners had fled, drew his sword and was about to kill himself. But Paul called with a loud voice, saying, "Do yourself no harm, for we are all here."

Then he called for a light, ran in, and fell down trembling before Paul and Silas. And he brought them out and said, "Sirs, what must I do to be saved?"

So they said, "Believe on the Lord Jesus Christ, and you will be saved, you and your household." Then they spoke the word of the Lord to him and to all who were in his house. And he took them the same hour of the night and washed their stripes. And immediately he and all his family were baptized. Now when he had brought them into his house, he set food before them; and he rejoiced, having believed in God with all his household. (Acts 16:25–34)

And we know that in all things God works for the good of those who love him, who have been called according to his purpose. (Romans 8:28 NIV)

Praying about difficult areas of your life

- Take some time to praise God for all the good things He has done in your life: for giving you family, friends, accommodation, food; for saving you from hell and setting you free from the past; for giving you hope and an eternal future with Him.
- Tell the rest of the group some of the promises God has made to you over the years.
- Pray about the situation you find yourself in, and even though you may not understand why certain things have happened, choose to ask God to help you and choose to trust Him.

- Pray a prayer of agreement with your group over those situations you want to change, asking God for faith to believe it will happen.
- Ask God for the resources you need to keep going until that change comes (patience, grace or hope, for instance).
- Ask God to show you what you can do in those situations, that will help show others something about Him.
- Ask God to use the situation you are in to bring people closer to Him and to help them.

Praying for neighbours

God intervenes in other people's lives in answer to prayer. Many have no one who ever prays for them. As you pray for your neighbours going through difficult times, you give God's Spirit freedom to intervene and change things for them.

- List some of the difficult situations your neighbours are in at present (keeping confidentiality).
- Pray together that God will intervene to change those situations.
- Think about the resources they will need at present to keep going, and pray that those resources will be poured out on them today.

Prayer:
Lord, we pray for our neighbours [list their names] going through difficult times. Please touch their lives with Your power: Your power to heal, Your power to release finances, Your power to bring reconciliation, Your power to bring lonely people into relationship with others, Your power to bring forgiveness, Your power to restore. Please move powerfully in all of our streets.
Amen.

Week 11: Praying with the Armour of God and for Evangelism

Finally, my brethren, be strong in the Lord and in the power of His might. Put on the whole armor of God, that you may be able to stand against the wiles of the devil. For we do not wrestle against flesh and blood, but against principalities, against powers, against the rulers of the darkness of this age, against spiritual hosts of wickedness in the heavenly places. Therefore take up the whole armor of God, that you may be able to withstand in the evil day, and having done all, to stand.

Stand therefore, having girded your waist with truth, having put on the breastplate of righteousness, and having shod your feet with the preparation of the gospel of peace; above all, taking the shield of

faith with which you will be able to quench all the fiery darts of the wicked one. And take the helmet of salvation, and the sword of the Spirit, which is the word of God; praying always with all prayer and supplication in the Spirit, being watchful to this end with all perseverance and supplication for all the saints – and for me, that utterance may be given to me, that I may open my mouth boldly to make known the mystery of the gospel, for which I am an ambassador in chains; that in it I may speak boldly, as I ought to speak.
(Ephesians 6:10–20)

For the word of God is alive and active. Sharper than any double-edged sword, it penetrates even to dividing soul and spirit, joints and marrow; it judges the thoughts and attitudes of the heart.
(Hebrews 4:12 NIV)

Paul describes prayer and evangelism as like being in a battle. He explains that there is armour to wear and a weapon to pick up. When we talk about putting on the armour in prayer, it's not about saying a special set of "magic" prayers to protect us. Each piece of armour is a lifestyle choice – a value we choose to live by every day.

Putting on the armour

Take some time to pray through the passage from Ephesians 6. Read each item of armour; then pray together that God will help you "put on" that value in your daily life.

Taking up the Sword of the Spirit

- Ask God to give you a verse from the Bible which you can pray over each of your neighbours (it may be the same verse for all of them or a different one for each person). Say a prayer for each neighbour based on that verse.
- Ask God to give you an opportunity to speak His Word into the life of one of your neighbours this week.

Prayer:
Lord, help us to be soldiers who never go to battle without our armour. Give us the courage to pick up the Sword of the Spirit and speak Your truth wherever we go, no matter how unpopular that may be. We pray for protection for every follower of Jesus in our neighbourhood, that we will be able to share our faith freely. We pray that every person in our neighbourhood will hear Your truth and come to faith. Lord, raise up evangelists in our neighbourhood, we pray. Amen.

Praying for neighbours

- Pray a prayer of agreement that your neighbours will hear the Good News and want to give their lives to Jesus. Be specific – pray for them by name.
- Pray especially for children in your street to come to know Jesus.
- Pray for churches doing outreach in your community.

Perhaps you could start thinking of ways you as a prayer triplet could take the Good News of Jesus to your neighbours...

Week 12: Praying Blessing

And the Lord spoke to Moses, saying: "Speak to Aaron and his sons, saying, 'This is the way you shall bless the children of Israel. Say to them:

"The Lord bless you and keep you;
The Lord make His face shine upon you,
And be gracious to you;
The Lord lift up His countenance upon you,
And give you peace.'"

"So they shall put My name on the children of Israel, and I will bless them."
(Numbers 6:22–27)

But I say to you who hear: Love your enemies, do good to those who hate you, bless those who curse you, and pray for those who spitefully use you. To him who strikes you on the one cheek, offer the other also. And from him who takes away your cloak, do not withhold your tunic either. Give to everyone who asks of you. And from him who takes away your goods do not ask them back. And just as you want men to do to you, you also do to them likewise.

But if you love those who love you, what credit is that to you? For even sinners love those who love them. And if you do good to those who do good to you, what credit is that to you? For even sinners do the same. And if you lend to those from whom you hope to receive back, what credit is that to you? For even sinners lend to sinners to receive as much back. But love your enemies, do good, and lend, hoping for nothing in return; and your reward will be great, and you will be sons of the Most High. For He is kind to the unthankful and evil. Therefore be merciful, just as your Father also is merciful. (Luke 6:27–36)

Blessing is a powerful concept in Scripture. As we speak good things over people in God's name, He responds by doing good things for them. Blessing can lift burdens, break strongholds, release prisoners, and comfort those in grief and pain. It's a privilege God gives His people: to do good to those around them by blessing them.

And Jesus says there is particular power in blessing those who aren't blessing us...

Blessing your neighbours

As you pray for each of your neighbours, think of one good thing you want to see them blessed with, then pray it:

In the name of Jesus I bless _____ with _____ today.
Amen.

Praying for those causing problems in your neighbourhood

- Pray a blessing over each person in your streets who makes life difficult for others in some way (parking badly, making excessive noise, getting into arguments with other neighbours etc.). Think of the most amazing blessing you could pray for them today, and speak it over them. Remember, blessing is not about getting them to do what we want; it's about speaking the good things of God into their lives. Give them to God and give Him permission to resolve the situation in whatever way He sees best.
- Pray for yourself, that God will give you grace to keep being kind to them, even when their behaviour causes you problems. Pray you will have wisdom to know how to relate to them.
- Also ask God to reveal if there is anything *you* might be doing that is annoying to your neighbours on your street.

Hopefully, after completing this twelve-week prayer guide, you are now ready to pray on your own. Please keep praying together, and keep praying even when you do not get an answer. It is our hope that you will now be more confident to pray together as a group without the need for more prayer guides. However, if you need more resources, they can be found on the www.neighbourhoodprayer.net website.

Week 13

Devise a week as a trial. Look back over the guide and reflect on the areas previously covered. You may want to do more prayer around a particular topic, or think of something new. Please tell us of any new sessions you devise, so we can share them with others in future editions of this guide on our website.

FORTY DAYS OF PRAYER

This prayer guide is intended to be used over the Lent period. We are also encouraging people to use it to take part in the #do1nicething campaign led by Love Your Streets (forty acts of kindness). Please see our website for further details and the article on page 61.

This prayer guide is a daily prayer guide, which may work best if used in the early morning, but which will fit into your daily life whenever you have a few minutes to spare. We expect the prayers to take no longer than fifteen minutes each day. There are intentionally only three prayer points per day so people don't get overwhelmed.

Safety

Children and vulnerable adults

This guide is not suitable for children or vulnerable adults to use because of its emphasis on getting to know neighbours. While the vast majority of people living on our streets would not harm a child or vulnerable adult, we are concerned about the growing issues surrounding abuse. We would ask you to be vigilant about this risk when interacting with your neighbours.

We strongly advise that, in getting to know your neighbours, you don't put yourself in a position where you are on your own with a child, vulnerable adult or someone of the opposite sex. We also ask that all adults adhere to the safeguarding policies of your local church, and inform your church leader that you are using this guide.

Day 1: The Power of the Tongue

> In the year that King Uzziah died, I saw the Lord sitting on a throne, high and lifted up, and the train of His robe filled the temple. Above it stood seraphim; each one had six wings: with two he covered his face, with two he covered his feet, and with two he flew. And one cried to another and said:
>
> "Holy, holy, holy is the Lord of hosts;
> The whole earth is full of His glory!"
>
> And the posts of the door were shaken by the voice of him who cried out, and the house was filled with smoke. So I said:
>
> "Woe is me, for I am undone!
> Because I am a man of unclean lips,

And I dwell in the midst of a people of unclean lips;
For my eyes have seen the King,
The Lord of hosts."

Then one of the seraphim flew to me, having in his hand a live coal which he had taken with the tongs from the altar. And he touched my mouth with it, and said:

"Behold, this has touched your lips;
Your iniquity is taken away,
And your sin purged."
(Isaiah 6:1–7)

- Pray for your lips to be clean; confess times you have gossiped about people or broken their confidence.
- Pray that you will be a neighbour whom people can trust.
- Pray for your neighbours, that all will be healed of past hurts caused by names they have been called, bullying, emotional abuse, or gossip both true and untrue that has been spread.

Prayer challenge: Speak only positive words about where you live and about other people, and stop being negative and complaining.

Day 2: Forty Days of Prayer and/or Fasting?

Then Jesus was led up by the Spirit into the wilderness to be tempted by the devil. And when He had fasted forty days and forty nights, afterward He was hungry.
(Matthew 4:1–2)

So [Elijah] arose, and ate and drank; and he went in the strength of that food forty days and forty nights as far as Horeb, the mountain of God. And there he went into a cave, and spent the night in that place.
(1 Kings 19:8–9)

So Moses went into the midst of the cloud and went up into the mountain. And Moses was on the mountain forty days and forty nights.
(Exodus 24:18)

- Ask God to reveal His heart for your street; pray over three houses on your street, ideally households where there are no Christians.
- If you live with other Christians, pray together with other members of your family.

Prayer challenge: If you are able, could you fast a food-group, the internet, TV, Facebook, phone calls for forty days? Or take it in turns to fast for twenty-four hours with other adults over a period of time? Please do not fast food if you are pregnant, diabetic, epileptic, on multiple medications, or if a doctor thinks it is unwise. While you are fasting, spend the time praying for your neighbours. Please go to www.ucb.co.uk/fasting for teaching on the nine types of fasting.

Day 3: The Harvest Is Plentiful, the Workers Are Few

After these things the Lord appointed seventy others also, and sent them two by two before His face into every city and place where He Himself was about to go. Then He said to them, "The harvest truly is great, but the laborers are few; therefore pray the Lord of the harvest to send out laborers into His harvest. Go your way; behold, I send you out as lambs among wolves. Carry neither money bag, knapsack, nor sandals; and greet no one along the road. But whatever house you enter, first say, 'Peace to this house.' And if a son of peace is there, your peace will rest on it; if not, it will return to you." (Luke 10:1-6)

- Pray to God for opportunities to get to know your neighbours; as you walk past your neighbours' houses, pray a blessing over their homes.
- Pray for all Christians and churches to be burdened to pray for their neighbours, their streets and the wider neighbourhood.
- Pray for Christians from many churches to work closely together to share the love of God with their neighbours so that they may have life in all its fullness (John 10:10).

Prayer challenge: Speak to other Christians and your leadership about praying for your neighbours. Consider setting up a prayer triplet as detailed on page 98.

Day 4: Honouring Parents

> Honor your father and your mother, that your days may be long upon the land which the LORD your God is giving you. (Exodus 20:12)

- Pray for all children in your street to honour their parents (whether the "children" are adults or minors) and especially for children growing up with a mother or father living elsewhere; help them to respect both their parents and also any step-parents, and pray for good relationships among family members.
- Pray that no child suffers any form of abuse and for healing for adults and children who have been the victims of child abuse at the hands of their parents. Help them not to feel condemned for their difficulties in dealing with how they feel about their parents.
- Pray for couples who would like to have a family of their own, but at this time are struggling to have children.

Prayer challenge: Try to get to know a single mum or dad, and offer them help and encouragement if you can.

Day 5: Fear and Discouragement

> This Book of the Law shall not depart from your mouth, but you shall meditate in it day and night, that you may observe to do according to all that is written in it. For then you will make your way prosperous, and then you will have good success. Have I not commanded you? Be strong and of good courage; do not be afraid, nor be dismayed, for the LORD your God is with you wherever you go.
> (Joshua 1:8–9)

- Pray for all those who are living in fear and anxiety about what the future holds, or the problems of tomorrow. Pray for them to be encouraged and for faith in God to replace fear.
- Pray that your neighbours will hear words of encouragement and kindness rather than discouragement.
- Pray that you and your church will be known for encouraging people.

Prayer challenge: Get a group together from your local church and prayer-walk the streets that you live on together. For prayer-walking guidance, turn to page 162.

Day 6: Praying for Your Neighbours to Know Jesus

> For God so loved the world that He gave his only begotten Son, that whoever believes in Him should not perish but have everlasting life. For God did not send His Son into the world to condemn the world, but that the world through Him might be saved. He who believes in Him is not condemned; but he who does not believe is condemned already, because he has not believed in the name of the only begotten Son of God. (John 3:16–18)

- Pray by name for three households on your street, that they would come to know Jesus as God's Son.
- Pray that opportunities will arise, now and in the future, to share what God has done for you.
- Pray that their eyes would be opened to who Jesus is.

Prayer challenge: Can you say hello to a neighbour on your street and strike up a conversation, with the aim of showing God's love to them through being a good neighbour?

Day 7: Showing Kindness and Love to Others

> ... His divine power has given to us all things that pertain to life and godliness, through the knowledge of Him who called us by glory and virtue, by which have been given to us exceedingly great and precious promises, that through these you may be partakers of the divine nature, having escaped the corruption that is in the world through lust.
>
> But also for this very reason, giving all diligence, add to your faith virtue, to virtue knowledge, to knowledge self-control, to self-control perseverance, to perseverance godliness, to godliness brotherly kindness, and to brotherly kindness love. For if these things are yours and abound, you will be neither barren nor unfruitful in the knowledge of our Lord Jesus Christ.
>
> For he who lacks these things is shortsighted, even to blindness, and has forgotten that he was cleansed from his old sins.
>
> Therefore, brethren, be even more diligent to make your call and election sure, for if you do these things you will never stumble; for so an entrance will be supplied to you abundantly into the everlasting kingdom of our Lord and Savior Jesus Christ. (2 Peter 1:3-11)

- Pray that you will be known for self-control, kindness and love towards others.
- Pray that acts of kindness will become common in your street and in your neighbourhood.
- Ask God if there is an act of kindness that He would like you to do on your street.

Prayer challenge: If you have not already started, could you visit the www.neighbourhoodprayer.net website and look at the daily suggestions for #do1nicething – for doing one nice thing per day? Also, if you are on Twitter, could you tweet the tweet for the day to encourage others to do the same?

Day 8: Prayer Rhythms and Peer Pressure

> And they went before the king, and spoke concerning the king's decree: "Have you not signed a decree that every man who petitions any god or man within thirty days, except you, O king, shall be cast into the den of lions?"
>
> The king answered and said, "The thing is true, according to the law of the Medes and Persians, which does not alter."
>
> So they answered and said before the king, "That Daniel, who is one of the captives from Judah, does not show due regard for you, O king, or for the decree that you have signed, but makes his petition three times a day."
>
> And the king, when he heard these words, was greatly displeased with himself, and set his heart on Daniel to deliver him; and he labored till the going down of the sun to deliver him. (Daniel 6:12–14)

- Pray for Christians who find it difficult to practise their faith because of pressure from family, friends or work colleagues who do not understand.
- Pray for all Christians in the local streets to pray more regularly and get into a habit of praying several times a day.
- Pray for God to teach all Christians and all who are not yet Christian that prayer works.

Prayer challenge: Pray for one of your neighbours, for a situation such as unemployment, illness, loneliness. Pray until something changes, and keep praying when you don't get an immediate answer. Pluck up the courage to tell your neighbour you are praying for them.

Day 9: Healing the Land

If My people who are called by My name will humble themselves, and pray and seek My face, and turn from their wicked ways, then I will hear from heaven, and will forgive their sin and heal their land.
(2 Chronicles 7:14)

- Pray that God will show you, either through research or directly, the sins that have taken place in the area you live in; ask God how to pray into these issues.
- Pray that God will put you and your church in touch with people who have experience praying in this area.
- Ask God to guide you in how to pray to heal the land.

Prayer challenge: Can you ask God to lead you to an area to anoint the land with oil as shown in Joel 2:19?

Day 10: Asylum Seekers, Refugees, Immigrants

> Take counsel, execute judgment;
> Make your shadow like the night in the middle of the day;
> Hide the outcasts,
> Do not betray him who escapes.
> Let My outcasts dwell with you, O Moab;
> Be a shelter to them from the face of the spoiler.
> For the extortioner is at an end,
> Devastation ceases,
> The oppressors are consumed out of the land.
> In mercy the throne will be established;
> And One will sit on it in truth, in the tabernacle of David,
> Judging and seeking justice and hastening righteousness.
> (Isaiah 16:3–5)

- Pray for all asylum seekers who are genuinely fleeing terrible situations in their home countries. Pray that your neighbours will have a generous heart towards those in need or to new immigrants living nearby.
- Pray for harmony between different faith-groups in your neighbourhood.
- Pray that God will improve your own attitude towards people from different cultures.

Prayer challenge: Could your family invite a family living nearby from another culture round for dinner? Or could a group of you get together to host a dinner? Or support a local charity helping asylum seekers in your village, town or city.

Day 11: Salt and Light

> You are the salt of the earth; but if the salt loses its flavor, how shall it be seasoned? It is then good for nothing but to be thrown out and trampled underfoot by men.
>
> You are the light of the world. A city that is set on a hill cannot be hidden. Nor do they light a lamp and put it under a basket, but on a lampstand, and it gives light to all who are in the house. Let your light so shine before men, that they may see your good works and glorify your Father in heaven.
> (Matthew 5:13–16)

- Pray that you will be the salt of the earth to your neighbours, leading a life that is attractive to others.
- Ask God to transform you so that you can be salt and light in your street.
- Pray to God that your home will become a house of prayer that will impact your street.

Prayer challenge: Ask God to show you and tell you what He would like you to do, now and in the future for your street and local area.

Day 12: Living Sacrifice

I beseech you therefore, brethren, by the mercies of God, that you present your bodies a living sacrifice, holy, acceptable to God, which is your reasonable service. And do not be conformed to this world, but be transformed by the renewing of your mind, that you may prove what is that good and acceptable and perfect will of God.
(Romans 12:1–2)

- Pray that you will come to love the Word of God and have a desire to read your Bible every day.
- Pray that you will find time to show love to those around you, and ask God to order your life so that you are not so busy that you can't spend time with Him and others.
- Pray for opportunities to help elderly neighbours living on your street.

Prayer challenge: Can you start to read more of the Bible each day, making this a daily habit?

Day 13: Unity among Christians

For I say, through the grace given to me, to everyone who is among you, not to think of himself more highly than he ought to think, but to think soberly, as God has dealt to each one a measure of faith. For as we have many members in one body, but all the members do not have the same function, so we, being many, are one body in Christ, and individually members of one another. Having then gifts differing according to the grace that is given to us, let us use them: if prophecy, let us prophesy in proportion to our faith; or ministry, let us use it in our ministering; he who teaches, in teaching; he who exhorts, in exhortation; he who gives, with liberality; he who leads, with diligence; he who shows mercy, with cheerfulness. (Romans 12:3–8)

- Pray for your church to have a strong relationship with other churches in the area, working together where possible and without competition or rivalry.
- Pray for all Christians living locally to be able to use the gifts God has given them and reach their full potential.
- Pray for Christians, living on your street and nearby, to forgive other Christians or their churches if they have been hurt.

Prayer challenge: If there is a Christian living close by, do something to show them love and encouragement; for example, send a card, flowers or a small gift.

Day 14: Hospitality

> Let love be without hypocrisy. Abhor what is evil. Cling to what is good. Be kindly affectionate to one another with brotherly love, in honor giving preference to one another; not lagging in diligence, fervent in spirit, serving the Lord; rejoicing in hope, patient in tribulation, continuing steadfastly in prayer; distributing to the needs of the saints, given to hospitality.
> (Romans 12:9–13)

- Pray that God will help you to practise more hospitality towards your neighbours.
- Pray for all the people who feel lonely on your street, especially those who are sick and unable to leave their houses and also have few visitors, if any, from week to week.
- Pray for eyes to see what is going on in your street, and to develop a heart for those living nearby.

Prayer challenge: Could you, together as a family or with some friends, invite a lonely neighbour round for tea and cakes?

Day 15: Bereavement

Bless those who persecute you; bless and do not curse. Rejoice with those who rejoice, and weep with those who weep. Be of the same mind toward one another. Do not set your mind on high things, but associate with the humble. Do not be wise in your own opinion. (Romans 12:14–16)

- Pray for all your neighbours who are mourning the loss of a loved one, either recently or in the last few years.
- Pray for healing for those who have developed depression as a result of their loss.
- Pray for all those who are so down that they are considering taking their own life; pray that they will be comforted; pray that they will find hope, love and a reason to live.

Prayer challenge: Together with two or three others, could you walk down your street and your friend's street, praying a blessing over every house in your street?

Day 16: Reconciliation

Repay no one evil for evil. Have regard for good things in the sight of all men. If it is possible, as much as depends on you, live peaceably with all men. Beloved, do not avenge yourselves, but rather give place to wrath; for it is written, "Vengeance is Mine, I will repay," says the Lord. Therefore

"If your enemy is hungry, feed him;
If he is thirsty, give him a drink;
For in so doing you will heap coals of fire on his head."

Do not be overcome by evil, but overcome evil with good. (Romans 12:17–21)

- Pray for reconciliation between neighbours or between members of the same family living on your street.
- For neighbours who cause difficulties, such as playing loud music, or who are argumentative, pray peace over their household and for grace from yourself.
- Pray for people you might struggle to get along with and that God will show you a way to bless them.

Prayer challenge: Is there anyone you need to apologise to or make a special effort to get along with, this week?

Day 17: The Police and Crime

> Let every soul be subject to the governing authorities. For there is no authority except from God, and the authorities that exist are appointed by God. Therefore whoever resists the authority resists the ordinance of God, and those who resist will bring judgment on themselves. For rulers are not a terror to good works, but to evil. Do you want to be unafraid of the authority? Do what is good, and you will have praise from the same.
> (Romans 13:1–3)

- Pray for your local neighbourhood policing team by name.
- Pray for the atmosphere on your street to be so full of the presence of God that crime rates fall, not just on your street, but on the surrounding streets.
- If you know of any neighbours who work in a position of authority, such as government officials or police officers, pray for them by name.

Prayer challenge: Find out the name of your local Neighbourhood Police Officer and send them a "thank you" card, and invite them in for a cup of tea if you see them passing by. Or could you consider setting up Neighbourhood Watch in your street (a secular organisation to help reduce crime)?

Day 18: Love for Your Neighbour

Owe no one anything except to love one another, for he who loves another has fulfilled the law. For the commandments, "You shall not commit adultery," "You shall not murder," "You shall not steal," "You shall not bear false witness," "You shall not covet," and if there is any other commandment, are all summed up in this saying, namely, "You shall love your neighbor as yourself." Love does no harm to a neighbor; therefore love is the fulfillment of the law. (Romans 13:8-10)

- Pray for an increase in love on your street and in your neighbourhood.
- Pray that God will show you how to be a better neighbour to those living on your street.
- Pray for opportunities to get to know your neighbours and show love.

Prayer challenge: Can you offer to go shopping for an elderly or ill neighbour?

Day 19: Blessing Your Neighbours

And seeing the multitudes, He went up on a mountain, and when He was seated His disciples came to Him. Then He opened His mouth and taught them, saying:

"Blessed are the poor in spirit,
    For theirs is the kingdom of heaven.
Blessed are those who mourn,
    For they shall be comforted.
Blessed are the meek,
    For they shall inherit the earth.
Blessed are those who hunger and thirst for righteousness,
    For they shall be filled.
Blessed are the merciful,
    For they shall obtain mercy.
Blessed are the pure in heart,
    For they shall see God.
Blessed are the peacemakers,
    For they shall be called sons of God.
Blessed are those who are persecuted for righteousness' sake,
    For theirs is the kingdom of heaven.

"Blessed are you when they revile and persecute you, and say all kinds of evil against you falsely for My sake. Rejoice and be exceedingly glad, for great is your reward in heaven, for so they persecuted the prophets who were before you." (Matthew 5:1–12)

- Pray for blessing on those who mourn, not just people who are grieving for loved ones they have lost, but also those grieving over injustice.
- Pray a blessing on the peacemakers, the merciful, the meek, those who hunger and thirst for righteousness.
- Pray for Christians who live on your street, that they will not be afraid to say that they are a Christian, and especially pray for those who may have fled persecution in another country for their Christian faith.

Prayer challenge: Could you tell a neighbour that you are a Christian, or at least not hide it, perhaps by wearing a cross or jewellery that represents your Christian faith?

Day 20: Miracles on Your Street

And they continued steadfastly in the apostles' doctrine and fellowship, in the breaking of bread, and in prayers. Then fear came upon every soul, and many wonders and signs were done through the apostles.

Now all who believed were together, and had all things in common, and sold their possessions and goods, and divided them among all, as anyone had need. So continuing daily with one accord in the temple, and breaking bread from house to house, they ate their food with gladness and simplicity of heart, praising God and having favor with all the people. And the Lord added to the church daily those who were being saved. (Acts 2:42–47)

- Pray for faith to believe, for wonders and signs to be done and to be seen in your neighbourhood, and for unity among local Christians and organisations.
- Pray for generosity towards those who have less among the people living on your street.
- Pray for God to add daily to local churches those who are being saved.

Prayer challenge: Ask God to place on your heart an area of your street you would like to see transformed.

Day 21: God's Heart for Your Neighbourhood

And the LORD God prepared a plant and made it come up over Jonah, that it might be shade for his head to deliver him from his misery. So Jonah was very grateful for the plant. But as morning dawned the next day God prepared a worm, and it so damaged the plant that it withered. And it happened, when the sun arose, that God prepared a vehement east wind; and the sun beat on Jonah's head, so that he grew faint. Then he wished death for himself, and said, "It is better for me to die than to live."

Then God said to Jonah, "Is it right for you to be angry about the plant?"

And he said, "It is right for me to be angry, even to death!"

But the LORD said, "You have had pity on the plant for which you have not labored, nor made it grow, which came up in a night and perished in a night. And should I not pity Nineveh, that great city, in which are more than one hundred and twenty thousand persons who cannot discern between their right hand and their left – and much livestock?" (Jonah 4:6–11)

- Pray for God to give you a heart, not just for a particular street that is connected to many streets which make up your village, town or city, but that He would give you a heart and desire to see the whole village, town and city transformed by God's power.
- Pray for people living on your street to repent of their sins.
- Ask God what your role is in transforming your street and village, town or city.

Prayer challenge: Pray for children to retain their innocence and have an encounter with God as a Father who loves them.

Day 22: Confession of Sins

Now on the twenty-fourth day of this month the children of Israel were assembled with fasting, in sackcloth, and with dust on their heads. Then those of Israelite lineage separated themselves from all foreigners; and they stood and confessed their sins and the iniquities of their fathers. And they stood up in their place and read from the Book of the Law of the LORD their God for one-fourth of the day; and for another fourth they confessed and worshiped the LORD their God. (Nehemiah 9:1–3)

- Pray for all the sins that you personally have committed and also for the sins of the people living on your street.
- Pray that all people will come to a revelation that they are sinners in God's eyes and that they will want to repent (say sorry and turn away from their sins).
- Pray for the people on your street to come to know what God wants of them and to draw closer to God.

Prayer challenge: Find a Christian you can trust, and talk to them about the things you really struggle with in life.

Day 23: Good Relationships with Others

Where do wars and fights come from among you? Do they not come from your desires for pleasure that war in your members? You lust and do not have. You murder and covet and cannot obtain. You fight and war. Yet you do not have because you do not ask. You ask and do not receive, because you ask amiss, that you may spend it on your pleasures. Adulterers and adulteresses! Do you not know that friendship with the world is enmity with God? Whoever therefore wants to be a friend of the world makes himself an enemy of God. Or do you think that the Scripture says in vain, "The Spirit who dwells in us yearns jealously"?

But He gives more grace. Therefore He says:

"God resists the proud,
But gives grace to the humble."
(James 4:1–6)

- Ask God for forgiveness for any selfish attitude or bad attitude in yourself.
- Pray for reconciliation within broken relationships on your street.
- Pray for those in bad relationships or broken relationships, especially those who feel rejected, that they will be helped to know God as a Father who loves them unconditionally.

Prayer challenge: Can you donate clothes, food or money to a local charity that meets the needs of those less fortunate than yourself? Or help someone through ACTS 435? (See page 182.)

Day 24: God's Victory in Your Street

Now Jericho was securely shut up because of the children of Israel; none went out, and none came in. And the LORD said to Joshua: "See! I have given Jericho into your hands, its king, and the mighty men of valor. You shall march around the city, all you men of war; you shall go all around the city once. This you shall do six days. And seven priests shall bear seven trumpets of rams' horns before the ark. But the seventh day you shall march around the city seven times, and the priests shall blow the trumpets. It shall come to pass, when they make a long blast with the ram's horn, and when you hear the sound of the trumpet, that all the people shall shout with a great shout; then the wall of the city will fall down flat. And the people shall go up every man straight before him." (Joshua 6:1–5)

- Pray that God will give you a strategy for praying for your street, so that His Kingdom will come and His will be done on your street.
- Pray for a heart of obedience so that you do what God asks you to do where you live.
- Ask God to make you hungry for prayer and praise, and to give you a heart to see all your street transformed by God.

Prayer challenge: Can you encourage some friends from church to come round and worship in your house, praising God and asking God to bless your street? Could you leave worship music playing in your home when you are out?

Day 25: Praying for Salvation on Your Street

But, beloved, do not forget this one thing, that with the Lord one day is as a thousand years, and a thousand years as one day. The Lord is not slack concerning His promise, as some count slackness, but is longsuffering toward us, not willing that any should perish but that all should come to repentance.
(2 Peter 3:8–9)

- Pray for every single house on your street, that not one of your neighbours would die without coming to know Jesus as their Saviour and God as their Father.
- Ask God to prepare the hearts of every person living on your street for a revelation of God.
- Pray for local churches to be prepared for new Christians to come into their church.

Prayer challenge: Is there a household in particular that God is asking you to focus your prayer on?

Day 26: Prejudice

My brethren, do not hold the faith of our Lord Jesus Christ, the Lord of glory, with partiality. For if there should come into your assembly a man with gold rings, in fine apparel, and there should also come in a poor man in filthy clothes, and you pay attention to the one wearing the fine clothes and say to him, "You sit here in a good place," and say to the poor man, "You stand there," or, "Sit here at my footstool," have you not shown partiality among yourselves, and become judges with evil thoughts?

Listen, my beloved brethren: Has God not chosen the poor of this world to be rich in faith and heirs of the kingdom which He promised to those who love Him? But you have dishonored the poor man. Do not the rich oppress you and drag you into the courts? Do they not blaspheme that noble name by which you are called?

If you really fulfill the royal law according to the Scripture, "You shall love your neighbor as yourself," you do well; but if you show partiality, you commit sin, and are convicted by the law as transgressors. For whoever shall keep the whole law, and yet stumble in one point, he is guilty of all. For He who said, "Do not commit adultery," also said, "Do not murder." Now if you do not commit adultery, but you do murder, you have become a transgressor of the law. So speak and so do as those who will be judged by the law of liberty. For judgment is without mercy to the one who has shown no mercy. Mercy triumphs over judgment.
(James 2:1-13)

- Ask God to cleanse you of any prejudices you have developed towards any people-group, social class or cultural difference.
- Ask God to help you treat all people equally and to show love to everyone regardless of how they speak, dress or act, and whatever their beliefs, even offensive beliefs.
- Ask God to help you and others living on your street to show mercy to others.

Prayer challenge: Is there a neighbour who is sick or in need of your help? Together with two or three others, could you visit them? Or buy them a small present or a "get well" card?

Day 27: The Church at the Heart of the Community

"Now, therefore," says the LORD,
"Turn to Me with all your heart,
 With fasting, with weeping, and with mourning."
 So rend your heart, and not your garments;
 Return to the LORD your God,
 For He is gracious and merciful,
 Slow to anger, and of great kindness;
 And He relents from doing harm.
 Who knows if He will turn and relent,
 And leave a blessing behind Him –
 A grain offering and a drink offering
 For the LORD your God?

Blow the trumpet in Zion,
Consecrate a fast,
Call a solemn assembly;
Gather the people,
Sanctify the congregation,
Assemble the elders,
Gather the children and nursing babes;
Let the bridegroom go out from his chamber,
And the bride from her dressing room.
Let the priests, who minister to the LORD,
Weep between the porch and the altar;
Let them say, "Spare Your people, O LORD,
And do not give Your heritage to reproach,
That the nations should rule over them.
Why should they say among the peoples,
'Where is their God?'"

Then the LORD will be zealous for His land,
And pity His people. (Joel 2:12–18)

- Ask God to forgive all local churches for the times they have failed to show love or meet the needs of their local community.
- Ask God to send His Holy Spirit in power to all of His people, that they may hunger and thirst for God in a new way.
- Pray for all attending church to develop a passion for prayer, and for church leaders to be surprised by the new interest in praying.

Prayer challenge: Ask others in your church to pray for a vision to reach the local community and for everyone's ears to be open to hear what God is saying.

Day 28: Deceit

Hear the word of the LORD,
You children of Israel,
For the LORD brings a charge against the inhabitants of the land:

"There is no truth or mercy
Or knowledge of God in the land.
By swearing and lying,
Killing and stealing and committing adultery,
They break all restraint,
With bloodshed upon bloodshed.
Therefore the land will mourn;
And everyone who dwells there will waste away
With the beasts of the field
And the birds of the air;
Even the fish of the sea will be taken away."
(Hosea 4:1–3)

- Pray for all your neighbours, that they would stop lying and being dishonest and stealing, including the pursuit in some cases of benefits they are not entitled to, or fraudulent claims for compensation.
- Pray for all your neighbours to stop committing sexual sin in all its forms.
- Pray that none of your neighbours will commit murder in their lifetime.
- Pray for your street to be cleansed of all past sins that have taken place and for the blood of Jesus to wash your street clean.

Prayer challenge: Spend the day, every time a negative thought comes into your head, turning the negative thought into a blessing.

Day 29: Generations

So the LORD said to Moses: "See, I have made you as God to Pharaoh, and Aaron your brother shall be your prophet. You shall speak all that I command you. And Aaron your brother shall tell Pharaoh to send the children of Israel out of his land. And I will harden Pharaoh's heart, and multiply My signs and My wonders in the land of Egypt. But Pharaoh will not heed you, so that I may lay My hand on Egypt and bring My armies and My people, the children of Israel, out of the land of Egypt by great judgments. And the Egyptians shall know that

I am the Lord, when I stretch out My hand on Egypt and bring out the children of Israel from among them."

Then Moses and Aaron did so; just as the Lord commanded them, so they did. And Moses was eighty years old and Aaron eighty-three years old when they spoke to Pharaoh.
(Exodus 7:1–7)

- Pray for everyone who is older and feels that their life is coming to an end; pray that God will give them a revelation for their life and the knowledge that they still have a huge contribution to make.
- Pray for the younger and the older generations living on your street, that they will respect one another.
- Pray for all those whom society considers elderly, that they will feel a new sense of energy and excitement about the future.

Prayer challenge: Is there an elderly neighbour you could help with gardening, shopping, DIY?

Day 30: Hypocrisy and Gossip

In the meantime, when an innumerable multitude of people had gathered together, so that they trampled one another, He began to say to His disciples first of all, "Beware of the leaven of the Pharisees, which is hypocrisy. For there is nothing covered that will not be revealed, nor hidden that will not be known. Therefore whatever you have spoken in the dark will be heard in the light, and what you have spoken in the ear in inner rooms will be proclaimed on the housetops.
(Luke 12:1–3)

- Pray that, in your own life, you will not be viewed as a hypocrite.
- Pray that you will be careful to speak only positively about people, so that, should you be overheard, you would not mind people hearing what you have said.
- Pray that your neighbours view you as someone who is trustworthy and never as a gossip.

Prayer challenge: If you have been guilty of gossiping about people, or saying negative things, ask God for forgiveness and from this day onwards aim not to repeat this mistake.

Day 31: Healing on Your Street

And through the hands of the apostles many signs and wonders were done among the people. And they were all with one accord in Solomon's Porch. Yet none of the rest dared join them, but the people esteemed them highly. And believers were increasingly added to the Lord, multitudes of both men and women, so that they brought the sick out into the streets and laid them on beds and couches, that at least the shadow of Peter passing by might fall on some of them. Also a multitude gathered from the surrounding cities to Jerusalem, bringing sick people and those who were tormented by unclean spirits, and they were all healed.
(Acts 5:12–16)

- Pray that you may be so filled with the Holy Spirit that your thoughts, words and actions reveal God to your neighbours, that your prayers are answered. and the atmosphere over your street is changed.
- Pray for God to heal people of any emotional, spiritual and physical problems.
- Pray that miraculous healings will start to happen in your street and that people will know God as a result.

Prayer challenge: If there is someone who is sick on your street, could you call together some Christian friends to pray for their situation? Could you tell your neighbour you are praying for them?

How I like to pray? I like to pray in tongues, as well as in my understanding, either quietly or loud, whilst kneeling, sitting, standing or prostrating on the floor as deemed fit.

Pastor Stephen Odularu, Manchester

Day 32: Being Selfless

Therefore if there is any consolation in Christ, if any comfort of love, if any fellowship of the Spirit, if any affection and mercy, fulfill my joy by being like-minded, having the same love, being of one accord, of one mind. Let nothing be done through selfish ambition or conceit, but in lowliness of mind let each esteem others better than himself. Let each of you look out not only for his own interests, but also for the interests of others. (Philippians 2:1–4)

- Pray for an increase in your love towards others, so much so that you are willing to sacrifice time watching TV, playing on computer games, or going on Facebook and Twitter.
- Pray for your street, that people will start to show love to one another on a new level, looking out for other people's needs rather than their own.

Prayer challenge: Can you ask God to highlight a way that you could be more sacrificial with your time?

Day 33: Following the Teachings of the Bible

Beloved, while I was diligent to write to you concerning our common salvation, I found it necessary to write to you exhorting you to contend earnestly for the faith which was once for all delivered to the saints. For certain men have crept in unnoticed, who long ago were marked out for this condemnation, ungodly men, who turn the grace of our God into lewdness and deny the only Lord God and our Lord Jesus Christ. (Jude 3–4)

- Pray for all Christians to remember what God has done for them through Jesus dying on the cross.
- Pray for people living on your street to have many opportunities to hear the gospel from your church and others.
- Pray that all Christians living locally would apply the teachings of the Bible to their own lives, impacting those around them.

Prayer challenge: Is there someone living on your street you might be willing to invite in the future to an Alpha course or a similar course about Christianity? Could you pray for them until the time is right to ask them? Wait for God to show you the right time.

Day 34: Knowing God

Come, and let us return to the Lord;
For He has torn, but He will heal us;
He has stricken, but He will bind us up.
After two days He will revive us;
On the third day He will raise us up,
That we may live in His sight.
Let us know,
Let us pursue the knowledge of the Lord.
His going forth is established as the morning;
He will come to us like the rain,
Like the latter and former rain to the earth. (Hosea 6:1-3)

- Pray for all the people living on your street, that they will dream dreams and have visions of God.
- Pray that they will know the awesome power that God has, enabling lives to change for good, redeeming impossible situations, providing solutions and helping at times of greatest need.
- Pray for the sudden realisation on your street of who God is and that He desperately desires relationship with every individual.

Prayer challenge: Ask God to show you specifically how to pray for three households on your street, in order to lead them to Christ.

Day 35: Life and Prosperity on Your Street

Along the bank of the river, on this side and that, will grow all kinds of trees used for food; their leaves will not wither, and their fruit will not fail. They will bear fruit every month, because their water flows from the sanctuary. Their fruit will be for food, and their leaves for medicine. (Ezekiel 47:12)

- Pray for new life to come to your street: where there is fear, let there be faith; where there is rejection, let there be love; where there is sickness, let there be healing; where there is crisis, let there be resolution.
- Pray for people suffering from financial problems and debts, who are finding it difficult to provide food for all the family, that they will experience a financial miracle; pray for prosperity to return to your street, affecting all the houses.
- Pray for all those who have been unemployed, that God would provide jobs and increase their sense of self-worth. Pray for the Holy Spirit to visit your street in power.

Prayer challenge: Do you have faith to pray for a revival to break out in your street, even if you have to pray for years?

Day 36: Sharing God's Story on Your Street

Jesus said to them, "My food is to do the will of Him who sent Me, and to finish His work. Do you not say, 'There are still four months and then comes the harvest'? Behold, I say to you, lift up your eyes and look at the fields, for they are already white for harvest! And he who reaps receives wages, and gathers fruit for eternal life, that both he who sows and he who reaps may rejoice together. For in this the saying is true: 'One sows and another reaps.' I sent you to reap that for which you have not labored; others have labored, and you have entered into their labors." (John 4:34–38)

- Pray that God will equip you to form deep relationships based on genuine love and concern for your neighbours, and that from these, opportunities to share your faith will arise.
- Pray that God will show you when and how to speak to your neighbours about your story, your journey with God; but pray for patience for God to reveal the right time.
- Pray for courage to be Jesus' representative in your street.

Prayer challenge: Are you willing to share your faith one day with your neighbour?

Day 37: Faith

But above all, my brethren, do not swear, either by heaven or by earth or with any other oath. But let your "Yes" be "Yes," and your "No," "No," lest you fall into judgment.

Is anyone among you suffering? Let him pray. Is anyone cheerful? Let him sing psalms. Is anyone among you sick? Let him call for the elders of the church, and let them pray over him, anointing him with oil in the name of the Lord. And the prayer of faith will save the sick, and the Lord will raise him up. And if he has committed sins, he will be forgiven. Confess your trespasses to one another, and pray for one another, that you may be healed. The effective, fervent prayer of a righteous man avails much. (James 5:12–16)

- Pray for more faith to believe that when you pray, your prayers will be answered.
- Pray for God to help you trust Him more.
- Stretch your faith by believing for the impossible on your street.

Prayer challenge: Knowing your neighbours' circumstances, ask God who you should pray for, in faith, for a breakthrough in their circumstances.

Day 38: Praying for Other Christians

I know your works, that you are neither cold nor hot. I could wish you were cold or hot. So then, because you are lukewarm, and neither cold nor hot, I will vomit you out of My mouth. Because you say, "I am rich, have become wealthy, and have need of nothing" – and do not know that you are wretched, miserable, poor, blind, and naked – I counsel you to buy from Me gold refined in the fire, that you may be rich; and white garments, that you may be clothed, that the shame of your nakedness may not be revealed; and anoint your eyes with eye salve, that you may see. As many as I love, I rebuke and chasten. Therefore be zealous and repent. Behold, I stand at the door and knock. If anyone hears My voice and opens the door, I will come in to him and dine with him, and he with Me. (Revelation 3:15–20)

- Pray that you and others will not become lukewarm Christians; pray that those who are lukewarm will realise their condition before God.
- Pray for everyone living on your street to have ears to hear if Jesus stands at the door and knocks.
- Pray for your neighbours who once attended church, but who somehow have lost their faith, to return to Jesus.

Prayer challenge: Can you walk your street praying a prayer of blessing over every household?

Day 39: Real Love

> Though I speak with the tongues of men and of angels, but have not love, I have become sounding brass or a clanging cymbal. And though I have the gift of prophecy, and understand all mysteries and all knowledge, and though I have all faith, so that I could remove mountains, but have not love, I am nothing. And though I bestow all my goods to feed the poor, and though I give my body to be burned, but have not love, it profits me nothing.
>
> Love suffers long and is kind; love does not envy; love does not parade itself, is not puffed up; does not behave rudely, does not seek its own, is not provoked, thinks no evil; does not rejoice in iniquity, but rejoices in the truth; bears all things, believes all things, hopes all things, endures all things. Love never fails.
> (1 Corinthians 13:1–8)

- Pray that you and others have genuine love for your neighbours, so that even if you see none of your prayers answered and not one of them becomes a Christian, you will continue to love them.
- Pray for those suffering from alcohol addictions and those involved in the sex trade, for the abusive individual, the drug addict, the criminal… pray that they too will be transformed by the love of Christ and as a result will not only be able to receive love, but show genuine love for others.

Prayer challenge: Can you commit to visiting a housebound neighbour (someone who cannot get out of the house because of illness)?

Day 40: Making Disciples

And Jesus came and spoke to them, saying, "All authority has been given to Me in heaven and on earth. Go therefore and make disciples of all the nations, baptizing them in the name of the Father and of the Son and of the Holy Spirit, teaching them to observe all things that I have commanded you; and lo, I am with you always, even to the end of the age." (Matthew 28:18–20)

- Pray that your life now, and for the rest of your days, is a living example of how to follow Jesus' teachings and that even if you never opened your mouth to say anything about it, people would recognise you as a positive example of what it is like to be a true disciple of Jesus.
- Pray that this would be true of all the Christians who live locally.
- Pray that God will move in power to transform your neighbourhood as more people become followers of Jesus.

Prayer challenge: Could you, with your church leader's permission and the help of many others, organise giving out the Father's Love Letter to everyone who lives in your postcode area?

Congratulations! You have prayed ten hours of prayer over the last forty days for your neighbours and all aspects of your community. Can you keep going? More prayer guides will soon be available online.

NEIGHBOURHOOD PRAYER DIARY

Introduction

"When I say 'hallowed be thy name; thy kingdom come,' I should be adding in my mind the words 'in and through me,' and so giving myself to God afresh to be, so far as I can be, the means of answering my own prayer." (J.I. Packer, theologian)

At Tearfund we have always held to the belief that prayer and action go hand in hand. They are intrinsic to one another. When we pray for something, not only are we calling on the Lord to intervene, but we should also be offering ourselves to God as His servants on earth – ready, willing and equipped to act.

Tearfund are pleased to partner with Neighbourhood Prayer Network, as we join with them to pray for our own neighbours and communities to be transformed. This call is echoed by our partners, churches and staff across the world as they confront big issues of global poverty and injustice in their own communities.

At Tearfund we are exploring the themes of Micah 6:8 as we reflect, pray and act. And just as prayer leads to action, we must start with reflection. And by "reflection" we mean a deep searching. Micah 6:8 TNIV says:

> He has shown all you people what is good.
> And what does the LORD require of you?
> To act justly and to love mercy
> and to walk humbly with your God.

We search the Scriptures for truth, we search God's heart for how we should respond, and we search our own thoughts to see if they correspond with the Lord's. And if they don't, we ask God to renew them.

But reflecting also requires us to seek earthly knowledge. What locks so many people into poverty, and what can be done practically to release them? Once we have a divine perspective combined with earthly knowledge, we can pray specifically and effectively. And those practical, Spirit-filled prayers will inevitably lead to action – because if we share God's concern and know how things can change, we are stirred to do something.

Our actions may be in our communities: we may be led to write to our MP, volunteer, or offer support and encouragement to local charities.

As we pray together, we do so with one voice, as part of a Global Poverty Prayer Movement. Be encouraged to think about ways that you can reflect, pray, and act in response. Because, when we pray, we're transformed, and – with God's help – we can transform our streets, our nations and the world around us.

Sara Kandiah, Tearfund Prayer Co-ordinator

Neighbour Statistics

- 59% of us feel we neither have a lot in common with, nor share, our neighbours' values.[8]
- 56% of people over 65 retain a sense of community spirit, enjoying spending time with neighbours,[7] being more likely to chat to neighbours, and trusting them to look after deliveries in their absence.[7]
- 20% of younger people (25–34) do not know the names of anyone in their street.[9]
- Across age groups, a survey from insurance firm Legal and General shows that most of us would only immediately recognise 1 in 3 people on our street.[8]
- 37% of us have never done anything for a neighbour and this rises to 47% in the 25–34 age group.[9]
- 61% of the nation never volunteer for a charity or community initiative.[9] The main reason given is a lack of time (63%), followed by work commitments.
- The average Briton watches 14 hours of TV with 17% watching more than 30 hours.[9]

Spiritual Statistics

- 69% of the churches in the UK do not have a dedicated weekly prayer meeting.
- A typical church in the UK is open less than 15 hours per week.

Bibliography (all sources can be accessed through Google):

1. David Rose, health correspondent, "Britain in the grip of epidemic of loneliness," The Times, 25 May 2010.
2. Sean Coughlan, BBC News education and family correspondent, "Loneliness is hidden killer of elderly" http://www.bbc.co.uk/news/education-12324231.
3. "Divorce rate lowest for 29 years," BBC website, 28 January 2010.
4. "One-parent families on the rise," BBC website, 11 April 2007.
5. Steve Doughty, "Nation of broken families: One in three children lives with a single parent or with a step mum or dad," 25 June 2010 www.dailymail.co.uk/news/article-1289399/nation-broken-families-onechildren-lives-single-parent-step-mum-dad.html/#ixzz1 b11 y8ck.
6. Rebecca O'Neill, Experiments in Living: The Fatherless Family (September, 2002).
7. "Do you know your neighbours?" BBC website, 4 December 2009.
8. Rebecca Smithers, "Neighbours: No one really knows their neighbours" survey, The Guardian, 16 August 2010.
9. "Bothered Britain" simplyhealth.co.uk/shcore/sh/content/pdf/surveys/bothered Britain-rep-feb-1 O.pdf.

Sunday – Church and the Community

Focusing on our church leaders, including deacons, elders, parish church council, greeters, ushers, worship leaders, choir, technicians, department leaders, maintenance and administrative staff. The other focus is where Christianity is found within the community: other churches in our area, hospital and prison chaplains, undertakers, street pastors, Christian charity leaders, and prayer ministries.

My Church	People to Pray for
Minister and/or Leaders	
Elders, Deacons & PCC	
Choir & Worship Team	
Ministry and Teaching Team	
Youth Team	
Mission Team	
Children's Work	
Admin & Maintenance Staff	
Greeters, Ushers and Servers	
Community Outreach Team	
Denomination Leader(s)	
Others	
Within the Community	
Other Local Churches	
Hospital & Prison Chaplains	
Christian Counselling	
Street Pastors	
Local Christian Ministries	
Christian Retreat Centres	
Other	

Monday – Work

Work life can be a cause of stress and frustration, so it is important to pray for work colleagues, supervisors, managers and owners, that God would prosper the work; that relationships in the workplace would be strong and positive for everyone involved. If you are currently out of work, then please consider praying for the people in your last place of employment or for the workplace of a loved one.

My Work Life	People to Pray For
Owner(s), CEO's, Directors	
Management	
Supervisors	
Receptionist	
Sales & Marketing Staff	
Production Staff	
Finance Staff	
Administration Staff	
Human Resource Staff	
Union Representatives	
Suppliers to the Workplace	
Customers of the Workplace	
People Making Deliveries	
Window Cleaners	
Office Cleaners	

Tuesday – Government and Economy

We should always remember to pray for those in authority: the leaders of our nation and our locality. We might disagree with their politics on occasion, but this should not stop us praying for them. And praying also for the economy. When God blesses a nation, we have the opportunity to be a blessing to other nations. Praying for a healthy economy helps us and others in many ways.

For Those in Authority	People to Pray For
Leader of the Nation	
Leader of the Government	
Political Party Leaders	
Members (MP, AM, SMP, MHK, TD)	
Civil Servants	
Local Councillors	
Mayor	
Army, Navy, Air Force Leaders	
Economy and Public Services	
Chancellor of the Exchequer	
Gas Supply Leaders	
Electricity Supply Leaders	
Leader of Tourism Board	
Unemployment Centre Leader	
Credit Union Leader	
Debt Counselling Leader	
Regional Development Leader	
Bank Manager	
Post Office Manager	
Telecoms/Media Provider	

Wednesday – Social Justice and Order

For being such wide subjects, social justice and order can mean very different things to different people. We have covered some of the institutions which ensure the provision of social justice and order. Please consider these wide-ranging subjects when you pray and, through the year, review who you are praying for as you identify other facets of social justice and order within your community.

Social Justice & Order	People to Pray For
Head of Police Services	
Neighbourhood Policing	
Local Magistrates	
Local Judges	
Local Council Leaders	
Citizen's Advice Centre Leaders	
Probation Service Leaders	
Youth Offending Projects	
Housing Association Leaders	
Victim Support Services	
Prison Visiting Organisations	
Drug Rehabilitation Centres	
Paramedic & Ambulance Staff	
Fire Fighters	
Coastguards & Lifeboat Crew	
Alcohol Abuse Counsellors	
Neighbourhood Watch Leaders	
Homeless Shelter Leaders	
Meals on Wheels	
Soup Kitchens	

Thursday – Arts, Culture and Media

Society is driven by the media and shaped by arts and culture. Society is constantly fed news of disasters, issues and problems, so it's important to pray for truth, righteousness and hope to feed through the media to society. Pray also for art and culture, that a constant recognition of the creativity God afforded us would be expressed there.

Arts, Culture & Media	People to Pray For
TV Channel Leaders	
Newspaper Editors	
Radio Leaders & Presenters	
Museum & Gallery Leaders	
Internet Website Leaders	
Local News Reports	
Local Advertising Agencies	
Local Library Managers	
Club, Pub & Bar Managers	
Concert Venue Providers	
Art & Craft Group Leaders	
Drama & Theatre Leader	
Music Teaching Leader	
Book Club Leader	
Cinema Managers	
Rural Festival Leaders	
Agricultural Show Leaders	
Village Fete Leaders	
Language Teachers	
Heritage Centre Leaders	

Friday – Families, Neighbours and Environment

Prayer for the family is fundamental for the Christian faith, praying for loved ones, young or old. We have also included friends in this section as close friends often feel like family members. The environment is also an important issue to pray for; we should do everything in our power to protect God's creation for future generations.

Family & Neighbours etc.	People to Pray For
Grandparents & Older	
Mother & Father	
Husband or Wife	
Brothers & Sisters	
Children	
Uncles, Aunts, Cousins	
Other Relatives	
Godchildren	
Close Friends	
Neighbours	
Family Help Organisations	
Family Counselling Helplines	
Christian Counselling	
Environment	
Local Farms	
Environmental Projects	
Countryside Management	
Climate Change Projects	
Animal Welfare Organisations	
Recycling Centre Managers	

Saturday – Health, Education and Sport

Health is a subject that can affect every one of us. You might have loved ones in hospital or nursing an illness. You might be providing a care service yourself. Think about everyone you might pray for. Within schools, for instance, there are Boards of Governors, head teachers, teachers, support staff, administrative staff, cooks, cleaners, gardeners, etc. And then of course there's sport!

Health, Education & Sport	People to Pray For
Hospital Leaders & Staff	
Surgery or Clinic	
Doctors, Nurses & Midwives	
Nursing Homes	
Residential Homes	
Carers	
Social Workers	
Counsellors	
Slimming & Diet Clubs	
Secondary Schools	
Special and Primary Schools	
Special Needs Units	
Nursery, Playgroup & Creche	
Local Colleges	
Universities	
Specialist Training Groups	
Sport Teams	
Sports or Leisure Centre	
Health Club or Group	

Visit www.tearfund.org/pray for more ways to keep connected in prayer.

PLANNING A PRAYER WALK TO BLESS YOUR NEIGHBOURHOOD

by Lyndall Bywater

This guide gives you practical tips on planning a prayer walk, as well as some of the theology of blessing which we would encourage you to draw on as you go out into your community. It ties in with the idea of praying blessing over your street which Adopt a Street are advocating. For a related article, please read the story of Ffald-y-Brenin on page 58 to see the power of praying blessing, and the transformation that results. Imagine what would happen if every Christian chose to continually pray blessing over a particular street.

This guide is suitable for children to use, providing they are accompanied by a parent or youth leader. Please adhere to your church's child protection policy.

1. What Is a Prayer Walk and Why Is It a Good Thing to Do?

> How beautiful on the mountains
>   are the feet of the messenger bringing good news,
> Breaking the news that all's well,
>   proclaiming good times, announcing salvation,
>   telling Zion, "Your God reigns!"
> (Isaiah 52:7 MSG)

A prayer walk is exactly what it sounds like: a walk filled with prayer. Prayer walking has been woven through the history of the British church for centuries. People would walk from cathedral city to cathedral city on pilgrimage, and these pilgrimages were all about prayer. Still today, many Anglican churches mark Rogation Sunday with a prayer walk around their parish boundaries. This tradition is called "beating the bounds," and is an act of claiming the ground for God in prayer.

Prayer walking simply involves walking around your community (either alone or in a group), praying for the places and people you see around you. You may plan to stop at specific locations, or you may just walk and see where the Spirit leads – either way, it's an exciting and engaging way to pray.

God told Joshua, "I will give you every place where you set your foot" (Joshua 1:3 NIV), and there is something powerful and significant about making our prayers physical: expressing our longings for places by going and standing there to pray.

Blessed to be a blessing

> ... Those who are led by the Spirit of God are sons of God. For you did not receive a spirit that makes you a slave again to fear, but you received the Spirit of sonship. And by him we cry, *"Abba,* Father." The Spirit himself testifies with our spirit that we are God's children. Now if we are children, then we are heirs – heirs of God and co-heirs with Christ, if indeed we share in his sufferings in order that we may also share in his glory.
> (Romans 8:14–17 NIV1984; see also Ephesians 1:3–14)

We are truly blessed. It is this amazing privilege of blessing which we want to invite you to use as you walk your community. This walk isn't about praying complicated prayers, tackling spiritual forces or solving social problems; it's about blessing your community with God's life, love and power. It's standing in your identity as a child of God, and speaking the good things of your Father's Kingdom into being in your local neighbourhood.

From the very earliest stories of God's interaction with humankind, we see a particular pattern of blessing emerging. God blessed Abram in order that he might give that blessing away to others:

> Now the LORD had said to Abram:
>
> "Get out of your country,
> From your family
> And from your father's house,
> To a land that I will show you.
> I will make you a great nation;
> I will bless you
> And make your name great;
> And you shall be a blessing."
> (Genesis 12:1–2)

Having blessed His people Israel, God expected them to extend His blessings to the foreigners in their midst:

> And if a stranger dwells with you in your land, you shall not mistreat him. The stranger who dwells among you shall be to you as one born among you, and you shall love him as yourself; for you were strangers in the land of Egypt: I am the LORD your God. (Leviticus 19:33–34)

Jesus continued that same mandate of blessing: no sooner had He won salvation and freedom for His disciples on the cross than He sent them out to carry this ultimate blessing to the very ends of the earth:

> But you shall receive power when the Holy Spirit has come upon you; and you shall be witnesses to Me in Jerusalem, and in all Judea and Samaria, and to the end of the earth.
> (Acts 1:8; see also Matthew 28:18–20)

The moment we open our hands to receive blessing from God, we are nudged by the Holy Spirit to go out and give it away.

This business of blessing is not just some well-intentioned positive thinking though. God's blessings are powerful and life-changing. They can unlock the stranglehold of death in desert places, and cause life to spring up:

> Instead of the thorn-bush will grow the juniper,
>   and instead of briers the myrtle will grow.
> This will be for the LORD's renown,
>   for an everlasting sign,
>   that will endure for ever.
> (Isaiah 55:13 NIV)

God's words can reverse the effects of sickness:

> The centurion answered and said, "Lord, I am not worthy that You should come under my roof. But only speak a word, and my servant will be healed."
> (Matthew 8:8)

God's words can bring impossible peace in the midst of impossible pain:

> Peace I leave with you; my peace I give you. I do not give to you as the world gives. Do not let your hearts be troubled and do not be afraid.
> (John 14:27 NIV)

> And the peace of God, which surpasses all understanding, will guard your hearts and minds through Christ Jesus.
> (Philippians 4:7)

When God speaks in blessing, the world is changed. And we, His children, are given the privilege of accessing those same blessings. We get to experience them in our own lives, but we're also given the privilege of speaking them into being for the people and places around us. Jesus gave His disciples authority to reverse the works of the enemy, and to cause life to spring up:

> I have given you authority to trample on snakes and scorpions and to overcome all the power of the enemy; nothing will harm you.
> (Luke 10:19 NIV; see also Mark 16:17–18)

He intended us not only to be present where there is pain and sin, but to speak out the blessings which will turn those situations around.

As we walk the streets of our communities, whether on our own or on a church prayer walk, let's resolve to be good news: to be those who carry the blessings of God in our thoughts, words and actions.

2. Planning Your Prayer Walk

Before you gather people, work out the route or general area you're going to walk (or drive). Either create a route-map for people to follow, or tell them to go wherever God leads them, but to stay within a certain geographical area. Ensure that those who have difficulty walking can still take part in the event, either by praying at base, or by having a short route to walk, with plenty of stopping points. Also, have a wet-weather plan: either ascertain whether people are happy to walk in the rain, or else use maps of the area and pray together somewhere under cover.

Prepare some ideas of locations or things people can pray for while out walking, such as GP surgeries, police stations, retirement homes, fire stations, local shops and the streets people from your church live or work on.

3. Getting Ready to Go Out

Since this is a walk of blessing, it is crucial to take time together to receive God's blessing in your own lives before you start walking. We all put barriers up from time to time, not allowing ourselves to truly absorb God's blessings into our own lives, but before we can truly bless others, we need to remove those barriers.

Ask the group to get into twos and pray "Aaron's Blessing" over each other:

> The LORD bless you
>   and keep you;
> the LORD make his face shine on you
>   and be gracious to you;
> the LORD turn his face towards you
>   and give you peace.
> (Numbers 6:24–26 NIV)

As they are prayed for, encourage each person to consciously welcome into their lives all that this ancient blessing contains. Also encourage them to invite God's cleansing and empowering in their own lives before they go out, and remind them to put on the full armour of God as they pray together:

> Stand firm then, with the belt of truth buckled round your waist, with the breastplate of righteousness in place, and with your feet fitted with the readiness that comes from the gospel of peace. In addition to all this, take up the shield of faith, with which you can extinguish all the flaming arrows of the evil one. Take the helmet of salvation and the sword of the Spirit, which is the word of God.
> (Ephesians 6:14–17 NIV)

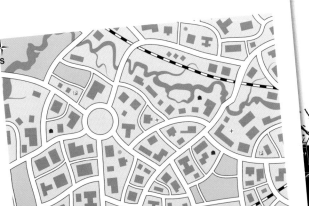

4. Practicalities of Prayer Walking

Send people out in twos or small groups, so that no one is walking alone. Groups should only be a maximum of four in size, so that it is easy for the members to hear one another when they stop to pray.

Remind the walkers that they need to be sensitive while they're out praying – not trespassing, not standing where they will cause an obstruction, and being considerate to those around them in the way they pray.

5. What to Pray For

Remind people to pray with open eyes and ears. Someone once said that prayer walking is "praying on site with insight." The fact of walking or standing in a particular place brings an immediacy to our prayers. We're not just imagining that place from the comfort of our prayer room; we're actually there – seeing it, hearing it, experiencing it – and that means God can speak to us through the things we see and hear there.

Make sure people take a Bible or a handout of Bible verses. Our prayers should be informed by our surroundings, but rooted in the Word. This is a walk of blessing, but we don't want to just make up the blessings we speak over our communities; rather we find them in God's Word. Those involved need to know what God's blessings are before they can speak them out. For example: "The Lord is your Shepherd, Castle Street! You shall not be in want" (based on Psalm 23); or "I speak over this hospital and say, 'Blessed are those who mourn, for they will be comforted'" (based on Matthew 5). Other useful scriptures for this would be: Deuteronomy 28; Ephesians 1:3–14; 3:14–21; Psalm 103.

Why not get the group to spend some time practising turning Scripture into blessing prayers? (For more prayers of blessings please visit our website.)

It's vital to be attentive to the Spirit: God is lavish in His blessing, but He is also strategic. He knows which particular blessing is needed in each place you will go to. So encourage the group to listen to Him as they walk, praying the prayers of blessing which He is prompting them to pray.

6. Physical Symbols

It can be helpful to have a physical symbol of blessing to use as you walk. Why not take with you some water and sprinkle a little bit on the pavement or brickwork of the places you bless? Please don't sprinkle water on people. (If you'd rather not use water, another idea would be to print stickers with an image or word of blessing on them and give people five or six each, to stick on pavements or brickwork as a sign of the blessing they've prayed.)

7. Finishing the Prayer Walk

It's always good to debrief after a prayer walk, and to share what you've heard God saying. So agree a rendezvous (either back at base or elsewhere along the route) and gather about fifteen minutes before the end of your time together. Give everyone in the group the opportunity to share, and pray for one another before you go your separate ways.

8. Making It More Than a One-Off

Once you've completed the walk, please encourage those present to make a habit of walking and blessing the places where they live and work. Perhaps challenge them to adopt a street or the street they live on, to walk it at least once a week, and to keep speaking blessing over it. Please see page 56 for the "Adopt a Street" article.

PRAYER REQUEST CARDS

You may want to produce prayer request cards to give out in our neighbourhood as part of a wider church campaign. The idea is that you either post a card containing a return address through the door, or knock on doors and hand the card to your neighbours. The latter is more effective as it helps you build relationships. We do not recommend you do this on the street that you live on, in case one of your neighbours is not happy. Most people are pleased to have the opportunity for people to pray for them. Normally, the prayer card states that you will pray for two weeks. Usually people then return the cards to a church address. A group then needs to pray over all the cards, keeping confidentiality.

Using Vista Print, a print and design website (www.vistaprint.co.uk), go to:

1. Business...
2. Folded business cards...
3. Browse design or Upload design.

Follow the steps, putting in your own information. See below for a sample:

PRAYER FOR TODAY: NEIGHBOUR FRIDAYS

Neighbourhood Prayer Network provides the Friday prayers and a neighbour challenge, all year round, in the UCB resource, *Prayer for Today*. We also feature an update of our activity here as well.

Natasha Ruddock writes:

The *Prayer for Today* was launched by United Christian Broadcasters (UCB) in May 2010 and is a companion publication to the *Word for Today*. This free resource is a quarterly magazine about prayer that features teaching, testimonies, prayer initiatives and local, national and global stories to encourage and equip people to pray more and reach out in their families, communities, cities, etc. The resource includes a prayer section which is used to pray daily for different aspects of the life of our nation and the work of UCB. Current readership figures (hard copy and digital) are over 20,000 people.

The aim of the *Prayer for Today* magazine is to encourage people to pray for change until we see transformation in our world. Each quarterly edition has a theme and we feature articles from Christians around the world. We partner with ministries such as 24-7 Prayer, Neighbourhood Prayer Network, Elim Prayer Network, Transformations Ireland, OneHope, Tearfund, Open Doors UK, Pray4Wales and World Prayer Centre. You can get the latest edition and subscribe to receive the daily prayer emails online at www.ucb.co.uk/pft. Follow us on Twitter @ucbmedia.

UCB PRAYERLINE
by Rachel Kerry

UNITED
CHRISTIAN
BROADCASTERS

"The problems seemed insurmountable to me, but with the UCB Prayerline I was able to cry out to God with the support of a Christian brother or sister when I needed this – a massive THANK-YOU. You all made a life difference to me." (Angela, April 2012)

Prayerline is a confidential telephone ministry of United Christian Broadcasters (UCB), where trained volunteers will pray for callers, in any situation, and invite God to bring His answer to their need. This service is not just for Christians; it is for all people, regardless of background. All of us, from time to time, face trials, temptations and difficulties; and our motto is "Praying with you, praying for you." We are not an advice or counselling service; we simply pray with our callers.

We took 112,250 calls in 2011. Of these calls, 2,351 were from people who were seeking Christ for themselves, a family member, or a friend. Prayers, in these cases, were offered so that people would become Christians. In addition, we also prayed with 3,307 callers for issues of depression and suicide.

Prayerline is manned by groups of volunteers in what we call "satellite groups," all over the UK. There are thirty-two Prayerline satellite groups with a total of 350 trained volunteers. They operate on a rota basis, covering daily from 9.00 a.m. to 10.00 p.m. throughout the week and with slightly more limited cover over the weekend. Each group covers the same time-slot each week. They operate from a room within a church building, and each team is overseen by a leader and has ongoing support from a satellite co-ordinator at the UCB headquarters. All volunteers are CRB checked and have full training from UCB staff before they operate on the phones. They also attend refresher training sessions.

Do you need someone to pray with?

Call UCB Prayerline on 0845 456 7729 or visit ucb.co.uk

UCB PRAYER

Prayerline also receives email prayer requests on a daily basis which are forwarded on to a team of volunteers to pray over these in their own homes. Similarly, for those who do not have computer facilities, there is a second team who receive the requests by post. Each of these is a non-contact form of prayer ministry.

Lastly, we also have a Forces Prayerline, originally set up for the families of the armed forces, but then extended to soldiers on active service, who are now able to access free calls to Prayerline from the actual battlefield anywhere in the world.

Contacting us:

- You can phone Prayerline for prayer on 0845 456 7729 (local call rate UK) or 1890 940 300 (local call rate ROI) or you can email a prayer via our website at www.ucb.co.uk/prayer.

- If you have, or know of someone with, a family member in the forces then we'd love to stand with you in prayer. You can call us on 0845 263 7223 (local rate call UK).

- We're always looking for more volunteers to join or set up satellite groups in their churches; and also to receive email prayers. If you are interested in knowing more then please contact us on 01782 764938, or email us at prayerline@ucb.co.uk for more information. Most satellite groups cover from three hours a week or more and our vision is to establish a 24/7 prayer service. You would receive full training, and equipment will also be provided.

- We also have Prayerline resources, such as bookmarks and business cards giving our details, which can be passed to family, friends and neighbours. You can order these by phoning 01782 764938, or by emailing us at prayerline@ucb.co.uk. You can also find us on our "UCB Prayerline" Facebook page.

FORCES
PRAYERLINE

WHEN YOU NEED SOMEONE TO PRAY WITH CALL...

Ops (Paradigm): *223
Germany: 0800 23 333 23
UK: 0845 26 37 223

Calls from Germany (landline) are free; UK calls are at local call rate (landline).

UCB
UNITED CHRISTIAN BROADCASTERS

INTRODUCTION

In this section, we want to highlight some ministries that are impacting city and town centres and the wider community in the UK. Recently, many housing developments in town and city centres mean that more and more people are taking up residence in these areas. These ministries appear to be flourishing at the moment and perhaps part of the reason for this is because they work across the whole spectrum of mainstream denominations, in unity. In this section we highlight the work of CAP, Redeeming Our Communities, Street Pastors, Street Angels, Foodbank, Acts 435, Healing on the Streets and also organisations that combat human trafficking.

CAP

Real poverty exists here in the UK and debt is a major contributor. For people who are living on very low incomes and struggling to make ends meet, dept repayments can mean they are unable to afford the basics of life: regular meals, heating, clothing or medication.

Christians Against Poverty has more than 200 church-based centres which help people with an award-winning debt counselling service while also giving people a chance to respond to God's love.

Single mum Joanne, aged thirty-seven, has chronic bone-disease and is paralysed from the waist down. She needed her home in Preston to be warm for both herself and her teenage daughter, who shares the same bone condition, and the cost of fuel bills tipped her into crisis.

"After my mum passed away I didn't know anything about running a household or paying bills," she said. "I have severe dyslexia and couldn't understand the numbers and letters. We had bad winters one after the other so it was very, very difficult. Most of my money was going on gas and electric.

So it was leaving very little for food and other items, and there were quite a few times when I had to go and ask neighbours if I could actually borrow food from them, a couple of potatoes or an onion. I was so ashamed. I was badgered all the time by the bank and other lenders. I was in such a mess."

Joanne's social worker recommended she call debt-counselling charity Christians Against Poverty who arranged for a home visit from the local church-based centre.

"They helped me immensely," she says. "Just in every way, emotionally and financially, and it was just such an amazing service." Interest payments were stopped as CAP negotiated with creditors, dealt with the paperwork and worked out a budget for Joanne.

"The first day I went to church was absolutely amazing. I went as a 'thank you' to Andrea [her debt coach] really, because I hated God at the time... but it was like coming home when I went through the doors. I started to get a sensation in my legs; now I can lift my legs and bend them. The doctors are baffled but I know it is God's plan. It's God who has done this for me so I can inspire other people with my story."

CAP is growing fast to help more people like Joanne, but it can't expand into new areas without the church. To find out how you can help, visit www.capuk. org or call 01274 760580.

REDEEMING OUR COMMUNITIES, DEVON AND CORNWALL

by Debra Green OBE, National Director

Over a thousand people packed into Plymouth Pavilions on 20 October 2011 for the launch event for Redeeming Our Communities in Devon and Cornwall.

Members of the public joined civic dignitaries, MPs, police and fire chiefs and officers, and an array of workers from voluntary and public sector organisations as well as faith groups, who all enjoyed an evening of inspiring community stories and live entertainment.

ROC brought together partnering agencies from Devon and Cornwall, working together to create safer, kinder communities, in a way that has not been seen in the region before.

Debra Green, ROC National Director, said that follow-up work should start as soon as possible. "One example of what can be done is the ROC café, a multi-agency youth project. We have seen ROC cafés established in many parts of the UK, and we want to see hundreds of these clubs. Police figures have reported up to 35% reduction in crime, in areas where ROC cafés operate. It's a youth club with a difference – with police, fire service, schools and churches working together with young people."

Since the launch, over fifty people from Devon and Cornwall have been trained as ROC Ambassadors to represent ROC in their own towns and communities, and lots of exciting progress has been achieved by local champions as listed below:

- In **Cornwall** – Bishop Tim Thornton of Truro circulated a letter to all Anglican churches in Cornwall encouraging them to respond to an offer from Probation to provide opportunities for Community Payback teams to contribute to local projects linked to the church – such as building projects. Probation have been really pleased with the response.
- In **Plymouth** – A ROC café opened in St Jude's on 26 April supported by police and other agencies. Fire, police and health services are developing a project called "Safer and Healthier Homes" which involves training church volunteers to visit homes of vulnerable people to facilitate access to support services where it is needed. They are also offering to provide training to voluntary groups, such as churches, that hold groups for older people, in order to deliver "memory clinics" to help slow the effects of dementia. Churches are being encouraged to adopt a residential care home, as part of a ROC of Ages initiative to provide pastoral support residents and staff. Derriford A&E department are looking to explore using youth leaders to support young people admitted with alcohol abuse.
- In **Torbay** – An event was held for those interested in supporting offenders to enable them to remain crime free. A project called "ROC Steady" is developing with training secured for volunteers under the Community Chaplaincy scheme (www.swcc-pi.org). Local police officer PC Tracey Sharam is linking with Upton Vale Baptist Church as part of an initiative to deal with those living on the streets. A ROC café opened on 22 March on the Great Parks Estate run by Riveria Life Church with £1,000 donated by the mayor and a £3,300 grant from Child Poverty Fund.
- In **Exeter** – The local police management team supported a ROC Exeter Launch on 21 June which was held in the Cathedral and attended by over 300 people. Plans are now in place to start up ROC projects.
- In **Ivybridge** – ROC has supported the launch of Street Pastors.
- In **Torrington** – A ROC Conversations event was held on 24 April with forty people attending to talk about youth and community facilities. Plans are progressing towards a ROC community centre.

If you are interested in any of the projects listed here, we would encourage you to contact www.roc.uk.com.

BEGINNINGS AND GROWTH OF STREET PASTORS
by Rev. Les Isaacs OBE, CEO

Street Pastors began in 2003 because, together with a core group of founding partners, I wanted to make a response to the rise in violent crime and antisocial behaviour in urban communities. We aimed to bring together the three forces in any town or city: the church, the police and local government. A few months later a small group of faith-filled Christians took to the streets of Brixton as the first Street Pastors patrol. Now, ten years later, almost 10,000 volunteers all over the UK offer practical help and care to vulnerable people who are out in city centres at night, whether they are partying and drinking or sleeping rough.

The mobilisation of these people, of course, comes after many years of prayer and relationship-building with churches and local councils. It comes after complex discussions with the police to establish a protocol agreement about safety and partnership. It also happens, week in, week out, because of the commitment of prayer pastors who come together at a local "base" to pray for street pastors and their community during the night-time hours of a patrol.

Through a radio link, prayer pastors keep in touch with what is happening on the streets and incidents that street pastors are involved with. Through prayer, street pastors have been directed to people who need help: the person lying unconscious out of sight in an alleyway; the teenager locked inside a nightclub toilet. Fights have been stopped and people calmed. Suicidal individuals have met someone who will listen to them and give them hope and encouragement. Many other tense situations have been diffused because people were praying.

Police highly commend the work of the church through the Street Pastors movement. As one officer said recently, noting the simplicity of the initiative, "It's not rocket science." I have to agree. It is simple and it works. I thank God that so many Christians want to make a positive difference to people and places and have been inspired by Street Pastors to persevere in their faith-filled commitment to engage with their community. There are others, many of them outside the church, who have been watching and waiting for the church to take action and for its "members" to make a practical expression of their faith in twenty-first-century society. Those people have said, "It's about time the church made its presence felt!"

I want everybody to see that Street Pastors works. Street pastors make God's love real to many people and they are enabled to do this through the prayers of prayer pastors. Prayer and action are strong partners.

STREET ANGELS

This article was written following an interview with Paul Blakey, MBE, CEO Christian Nightlife Initiatives

Street Angels started in Halifax when Churches Together began looking at the needs of the town and realised that the town centre on Friday and Saturday night represented a culture of binge drinking, violence, sexual assault, underaged drinking and was effectively a no-go area from 6.00 p.m. Twenty churches representing Roman Catholics, Anglicans, Methodists, Baptists, the United Reformed Church, New Testament of God, King's Church (New Church) and Elim, were in this group.

With the idea of launching a night café that would be open on Friday and Saturday nights to look after the vulnerable, this group contacted the police, who were very excited, commenting that it is recognised nationally that when the church works in a local area, amazing results happen. On the first night there were fifty volunteers and so they took to the streets, and Street Angels was born.

One particular story stands out in Paul's mind. Two fourteen-year-old girls were seen going into a notorious nightclub, and about fifteen minutes later there was a call to the club (the police and council had arranged for a radio link to Street Angels). One of the girls had "passed out" in the toilet and the other one had been carried into an alleyway. An ambulance was called for the girl in the toilet, but the girl in the alleyway was looked after by Street Angels and taken to safety in the café. One of the Street Angels happened to know the girl and identified her as being aged fourteen. Phoning her parents, it became clear that there were relationship difficulties due to her behaviour. Five years later the same girl came up to the Street Angels in the town and said, "You won't remember me, will you?" They were able to relay back to her what had happened that night. She told them how that night had changed her life and made her realise where her life was going. With the help of others and a Street Angel volunteer, she settled down, stopped drinking and going out, and was now at university.

Christian Nightlife Initiatives was launched in 2008, supporting and resourcing new and existing projects. In 2012 there are 120 local projects ranging from patrol projects such as Street Angels to Town Pastors and Night Light (Northern Ireland projects). Other projects include club angels, detached youth work, red-light district work (lap-dancing chaplains). These projects all work from 5.00 p.m. to 6.00 a.m.

Halifax, where Street Angels began, was the first small town to receive the "Purple Flag." The Purple Flag is awarded by an association of town centre managers and represents a safe and vibrant night-time economy. Halifax has kept this flag for the last three years. Since Street Angels and other projects began, Halifax is now a place where you can go out to the theatre until 2.30 a.m., there are coffee bars and restaurants, and there is less of a binge-drinking culture.

Since Street Angels has been working in Halifax, there has been a 57% reduction in crime. Nationally, the Christian Nightlife Initiatives was awarded the Big Society Award. Street Angels is similar to Street Pastors and they try not to work in the same town unless a huge city or area needs to be served. They choose to co-operate rather than compete, work in unity rather than disunity, honour rather than dishonour. Perhaps this is a lesson for all of us. It is also not a coincidence that this project was born out of "churches working together"!

ACTS 435: NOW WE'RE ALL NEIGHBOURS

by Jenny Herrera

Jesus said, "Love your neighbour" (Matthew 22:39 NIV), and surely the first place to turn is to those who live down our street. Perhaps there is something we can help them with. And yet, the sad truth is that we often do not even know our neighbours, let alone know what they might need, whether it is those in our street, village or town, or those further afield, struggling and requiring urgent support.

Patron Dr John Sentamu with Executive Director Jenny Herrera

ACTS 435 is a revolutionary online-giving charity that seeks to connect those in need with those who want to help, through the wonderful world of the internet. Its power and effectiveness comes from the way it operates, through the network of churches. Take Lorraine (name changed to protect confidentiality), who wrote directly to patron Dr John Sentamu, the Archbishop of York, in January 2012, citing her need for a sewing machine to improve her employment prospects.

By putting Lorraine in direct contact with one of the ACTS 435 participating churches in nearby Middlesbrough, a request was soon loaded up on the ACTS 435 website (www.acts435.org.uk). Donors from different parts of the UK responded and within a month Lorraine had her new sewing machine. She was full of gratitude for the "kind and urgent attention" to her request and the effort put in by the local advocate.

ACTS 435 is all about heart-warming stories like this. Take the Hadaway family in Scarborough, expecting twins with a serious health condition requiring twice-weekly scans in Leeds. How could their tight budget cover the extra petrol for the hospital trips? Through local church St Mary's, £100 from ACTS 435 was donated, which significantly helped to ease the burden on the young family.

The Hadaway family, helped by ACTS 435

Churches operating ministries to people in need often find themselves overwhelmed by the level of help required, in spite of their best efforts. River of Life Community Church in Suffolk runs a food and furniture bank but still found need outstripping local resources. By posting requests on the ACTS 435 website, over £4,000 has been used to benefit individuals and families in that church's local community.

It is all thanks to generous donors from across the UK who, through making financial gifts, are loving their neighbour in that wider sense. And donors love the fact that 100% of their donation goes in its entirety to the individual in need.

FOODBANK, NEWHAM by Pastor Tunde Adefioye

The Newham Foodbank was formed in March 2010 and started operations in June of that year. The sixtieth foodbank in the UK, the Newham Foodbank was set up by the Trussel Trust, in partnership with City Chapel, to provide emergency services to people in need, specifically by way of providing dry-pack food, enough for at least three days.

A foodbank is a type of storehouse which receives long shelf-life packaged/tinned foods donated by the local community, churches, schools, shops etc. We started from the premises of City Chapel on Tollgate Road, Beckton, and in the beginning we expected to feed about twenty people in one month, as this was what we considered to be the need levels in the community at that time.

However, we quickly realised that the level of need far exceeded our projections. Between June and December 2010, we fed 550 people with over 2 tons of food! That is about eighty people per month. By December 2011, we had fed our two thousandth person.

Our primary aim is to combat the effects of income deprivation and poverty in our community by offering practical and immediate support. This is in line with our identity and objective, which is to serve the community that we are placed in by making a difference in the lives of those in crisis. We do this in the following ways:

1. We work in partnership with local statutory agencies – such as children's centres, GP surgeries, charities and churches – which assess people's needs and refer them to us with pre-issued vouchers to visit our Distribution Centre. Here we operate a café-style environment offering drinks and light snacks, a listening ear, prayers, counselling and further referrals with consent, while food is being bagged for the visitors. We also provide a home delivery service for housebound clients or those who can't afford the travel fare or have young children. We offer a one-stop access point to a multi-agency platform (debt counselling, advocacy, health services etc).

2. We provide at least three days' supply of packed food, enough to provide ten balanced meals for an individual or family in need. Three days is the period assessed as the minimum time it takes for the appropriate agencies to be in a position to assist. In periods of delay in assessment, we are able to provide packed food for up to two weeks. We also have a unique scheme of providing holiday packed food to families who have children, as such families living in poverty are often unable to provide healthy meals for their children during the school holiday when school dinners, which are the major source of meals for most children, cannot be accessed.

3. We support socially disadvantaged or vulnerable people through the "Support Volunteer Scheme." This project allows those who have been unable to work in the community to be involved on a number of levels, whatever their ability. The aim is to improve employability levels, self-confidence and accredited qualifications, and provide employment for some in various sections such as the warehouse, at the Distribution Centre, and at supermarket collections. Volunteers are also involved in a wide range of supervised appointments, particularly in the centre, where they are involved in "signposting" and helping others in similar positions by speaking from personal experience.

4. Through City Chapel, we also have a group of volunteers called the "Support Group." This group provides a more personalised support for the clients of the foodbank, beyond the provision of food. While clients are waiting for their food to be packed, members of the Support Group sit with them, share a cup of tea, and seek to determine what might have caused the problem they are in. We will offer prayer and counsel if the client asks for or consents to it. Where there are issues beyond our remit, we will signpost clients to relevant agencies who may be able to provide them with professional assistance.

Two lives changed for the better by the work of Newham Foodbank:

- Serena, a young mum caring for two young children and her niece, was referred by Alternatives Trust, a charity based in East London. She was facing difficulties and had bailiffs chasing her for payment of debts. She was struggling between feeding herself and the children, procuring baby essentials like nappies, and keeping the bailiffs away. We were able to offer support by providing meals for herself and the children, and also offering advice and guidance on routes to the future, which freed up some cash. She was then able to negotiate with the bailiffs to accept a repayment amount based on her circumstances. She is feeling positive and ready to go back to her career as a hairdresser. In her own words: "Without the Newham Foodbank packs I don't know how I would have put food on the table or had extra money to buy nappies, pay for after-school childcare for my daughter, pay the bailiffs, or even think of the future."

- Mike is a pensioner who lives in sheltered accommodation and was struggling with paying his bills and purchasing healthy food to eat. The foodbank was able to provide an avenue whereby he is now able to receive food to tide him over during the periods when all the bills come at once, so he doesn't have to worry. In Mike's words: "I'm glad the foodbank was there to help me when I needed help and support."

HEALING ON THE STREETS

Healing on the Streets was birthed in Causeway Coast Vineyard Church, Northern Ireland, in April 2005. Since then it has rapidly spread across the UK and beyond. The first testimony is taken with kind permission from the website www.healingonthestreets.com. The second testimony is from Alistair Kay from Derby.

Carole Linton writes:

Having been on the "Healing on the Streets Team" since the outset, I have seen God move in a powerful way, in my life and in the lives of those I have been privileged to pray with.

The first day was one of mixed emotions. I was looking forward to doing God's work, yet having lived in Coleraine all my life I wasn't sure how my friends, work colleagues etc., would react. I found the experience challenging at the start, but now I can't wait for Saturday to come, so that I can get "out there" and pray with people.

When you see miracles taking place in front of your eyes, you want to jump up and down and tell everyone. To see legs growing, twisted fingers being straightened, fibromyalgia disappearing, being told of cancerous growths vanishing from scans and X-rays, and doctors left scratching their heads... you know that God is merciful.

I believe what we have experienced so far in Coleraine is only the start of much more. We are waiting expectantly for an even greater move of God. I work in a local school, and now pray regularly with both staff and pupils for healing, and have seen wonderful things happen.

One Saturday afternoon, while walking with my husband in a local forest, we met a lady who was suffering with back pain. We started to talk to her and had the opportunity to pray with her there in the middle of the forest. I personally have developed a deep sense of compassion for people who are hurting, and use my God-given gifts to speak into their lives, and to pray with them.

I hope that when you read this you will be encouraged to take that step of faith, trusting God for more, and consider praying with others for healing.

Alistair Kay writes:

I first met Kath and Phil at Healing on the Streets one day while they were waiting outside the Westfield Centre in Derby. They had their thirty-year-old son Mark with them. Mark was grossly overweight and sulked on his chair, looking scared and depressed.

I approached the family and asked, "Are any of you in need of prayer for healing?"

The husband and wife both said (in a thick Derbyshire accent), "Well, only God can sort 'im aht coz we've tried everything, me duck."

So I chatted to Mark and he explained that he was agoraphobic and alcoholic and that this was the first time out of his house in seven months. We prayed against the oppression and prayed into the alcoholism. They then left.

One month later all three were back at the Healing on the Streets spot. Mark, Mum and Dad were beaming. I said to Mark, "What happened to you?"

"It were amazing," he said. "I got home and opened t' can of super lager and for some reason I couldn't swaller it or owt."

He had been "dry" for three and a half weeks and, more than that, was now going out alone without Mum and Dad and was considering getting a job.

The transformation was incredible.

If you want to set up Healing on the Streets in your area, please contact **www.healingonthestreets.com.**

Alistair Kay

THE POWER OF SAYING "THANK YOU"

In 1998, posters were placed in police stations across Manchester. The message was positive and powerful:

REDEEMING
OUR COMMUNITIES

> To all police officers and civilian employees of our local police: Thank you for serving our society with commitment, diligence and integrity. Thank you for affording protection to the vulnerable, and for your efforts to maintain law and order for the benefit of all people in our region. We are praying for you: that God would be with you in your work and in your leisure, that God would protect you and your families physically and spiritually, that you would know Christ's peace in your hearts and minds. With love and appreciation on behalf of the whole Christian community in this area.

Debra Green OBE, National Director of Redeeming Our Communities, writes:

> This was much more significant than we realised at the time and led to a partnership between the police and the churches which has grown in Manchester and become a model now adopted in many cities and towns across the UK.

Neighbourhood Prayer Network, in partnership with Redeeming Our Communities, is proposing that churches across the country not only say "thank you" to the police, but to healthcare workers, to politicians, to the fire brigade, to cleaning staff, to the postman, to the bus driver, to people in all walks of life whom we meet each day. Let Christians become known in this country for saying positive words rather than negative ones, bringing encouragement where there is discouragement, bringing hope in a time of fear.

During October 2012 we are asking that people consider sending a "thank you" card, along similar lines to the message above, to as as many public sector workers as possible. Please use #saythanku on Twitter when tweeting.

Please visit www.neighbourhoodprayer.net or www.roc.uk.com

TO ALL OF THE EMERGENCY SERVICES THANK YOU!

HUMAN TRAFFICKING
Facts and Stats

- Worldwide, more than 800,000 men, women and children are trafficked every year.
- 77% are women.
- 87% of trafficked victims are sexually exploited.
- This is a worldwide criminal activity with annual profits estimated to be $32 billion.
- In the human trafficking market, a woman can be bought for between £500 and £8,000 – that's somewhere between the cost of a computer and a small car.

Jesus, God-made-man, rose to life again so that no one would ever have to live in slavery, and so that no one would ever have to be bought and sold like a commodity. He set the bar for what we're worth, and He is angered and grieved every time one of us is treated as though we're worth less than life itself.

And now He's looking for people who will stand up and fight to see the evil trade of human trafficking ended forever. Will you take the challenge? Will you pray and act?

(Taken from The Salvation Army's "Cut It Out" campaign against human trafficking)

How Do I Pray?

1. **Deliverance from slavery (Psalm 10:17–18):** 27 million people are enslaved globally in various forms of sexual and labour exploitation. Pray: "Loving God, forgive us that we, the human race, have allowed such an evil trade to grow so strong in Your world. Deliver all those who have been taken captive for the pleasure and convenience of others."
2. **Protection for the poor (Psalm 82:3–4):** People usually end up being trafficked as an escape from poverty, either for themselves or their families. Pray that children living in poverty will be protected from the lure of the traffickers. Pray that the family of God will reach out to meet their needs so they don't look elsewhere.
3. **Mercy for perpetrators (Joel 3:3):** All over the world, men and women are making money by selling others into slavery. Pray that they will be deeply convicted about the wrong they do, and that they will repent and leave this trade behind. Pray that their schemes will be exposed, and that every one of their victims will be rescued.

4. **Demand and supply (Leviticus 19:29):** Pray for your own local community, that the commercial sex trade will completely close down, so that there is no longer any market for trafficked victims. Pray for our national government, that it will make just and compassionate decisions which make trafficking more and more difficult in this country.

(Adapted from the Worldwide Evangelical Alliance's Anti Human Trafficking Taskforce Prayer Points http://www.worldevangelicals.org/human-trafficking-gts/ ongoing-projects.htm and first published in UCB's Prayer for Today in July 2012)

What Can I Do?

- **Be alert:** If you think you have met someone who may have been trafficked into sexual exploitation, forced street crime, domestic servitude or forced labour, please contact your local Police (do not use an emergency number, unless a crime is in progress).
- **Get informed:** Stop the Traffik have produced a fold-away leaflet which lists the signs to look out for if you suspect that someone has been trafficked. It's called "Spot the Traffik" and can be downloaded for free at: http://www.stopthetraffik.org/campaign/communities/what-you-can-do/20.
    - **Start or join an ACT Group:** Active Communities against Trafficking (ACT) groups are an initiative of Stop the Traffik. They are groups of people who meet together regularly to look at how they can reduce human trafficking in their area.

To find out more, visit http://www.stopthetraffik.org/campaign/ communities/what-you-can-do/31.

Behold what manner of love the Father has bestowed on us, that we should be called children of God! Therefore the world does not know us, because it did not know Him.

1 John 3:1

INTERNATIONAL NEIGHBOURS

Dinner4Good

DINNER4GOOD

Dinner4Good is an online system that helps charities raise much-needed funds by encouraging their supporters to have their friends to dinner. Neighbourhood Prayer Network thinks this is a wonderful idea and hopes that people across the country will consider inviting their neighbours around for a Dinner4Good – to raise money for charities such as Samaritan's Purse or Tearfund.

At Christmas our neighbours are keener to go to parties and raise money for Christmas, and are most open to the gospel. A Dinner4Good provides an opportunity to meet for a meal. In the case of Samaritan's Purse, we are proposing that a Dinner4Good becomes a shoebox-packing party. Shoeboxes must be taken to a delivery point before 18 November.

Samaritan's Purse and Tearfund both have pages listed in the Dinner4Good website; these are: www.dinner4good.com/SamaritansPurse and www.dinner4good.com/Tearfund.

Samaritan's Purse and Tearfund have provided examples below of some of the international work that they do. While Neighbourhood Prayer Network focuses on our immediate neighbours, we believe this should not be to the detriment of our overseas neighbours.

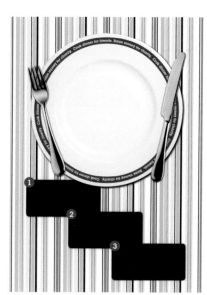

Dinner4Good is run by Bryan Sergeant, who explains how it works:

> Having friends to dinner is a nice alternative to running a marathon or jumping from an airplane.
>
> Dinner4Good makes it easy and discreet – your dinner guests can donate using their credit cards and you don't have to handle cash donations.
>
> To support your favourite charity, go to one of their web addresses (above) and follow the instructions. It takes about five minutes to send e-invitations to your friends. Your guests can then RSVP and donate online... and you all can see who's coming to the dinner and the total amount that's been raised.
>
> Dinner4Good handles all the donations and Gift Aid, so your charity typically ends up with 112% of the amount that's been donated.
>
> And some of your guests may hold a Dinner4Good of their own!

OPERATION CHRISTMAS CHILD

Since 1990, Operation Christmas Child, an initiative of Samaritan's Purse, has been blessing underprivileged children around the world with gift-filled shoeboxes, wrapped and packed by adults and children in the UK. Running between September and November, it is the UK's largest children's Christmas appeal.

The idea is simple: children and adults wrap and pack empty shoeboxes filled with little gifts; then Samaritan's Purse send them overseas and ensure they are distributed through local churches to children, on the basis of need alone. Each shoebox is an unconditional gift, with nothing asked in return.

In many cases, children receiving shoeboxes are also offered a copy of "The Greatest Gift," an illustrated booklet of Bible stories, handed out alongside their shoebox.

In addition, in a number of countries local churches invite these same children to attend a twelve-lesson follow-up course called "The Greatest Journey," where they can find out more about Jesus and have the chance to accept Him into their lives. The course is offered free of charge to children, without any obligation to attend, enabling them to relate to the gospel through Bible stories and interactive Bible teaching. Training teachers, providing resources and equipping churches to take the children through The Greatest Journey costs just £4 per child.

In 2011, over 700,000 children enrolled in The Greatest Journey in some of the world's hardest-to-reach places. At the time of writing, 388,000 of these children have completed the programme, with 260,000 children giving their lives to Christ. The programme has been implemented in fifty-four countries and has been translated into twenty-one different languages. Our hope is that every child receiving a shoebox will have the opportunity to participate in The Greatest Journey, should they wish to. Please visit www.samaritans-purse.org.uk/the-greatest-journey for further information.

Note: *Shoeboxes must be taken to a drop-off point before 18 November.*

To get involved in Operation Christmas Child, please visit www.operationchristmaschild.org.uk.

A Life Touched

Thembani is eleven years old. His mother and father passed away about five years ago, so Thembani now lives with his eight brothers and sisters high up in the hills of rural Swaziland, near South Africa.

When Operation Christmas Child came to his village, Thembani and each of his brothers and sisters received a shoebox filled with presents.

"I really enjoyed opening the box," said Thembani. "I've never received anything like this before."

Thembani's favourite gifts were his notebook, pens, and socks. "I love the notebook," he says. "I am going to write in it all the time."

An hour after the shoebox distribution, Thembani sat in the doorway of his hut, avidly drawing and writing in his new notebook. When asked how he felt about the gifts, he said, "I'm so happy, I'm tongue-tied!"

The gift that Thembani received was more than just a shoebox. It was the gift of education supplies, and toys so he could be a child again. It was also the gift of love at Christmas, and the gift of hope for the future.

The hope is there because the same church that brought Thembani his shoeboxes has also been supported by Samaritan's Purse to care for Thembani and his siblings – providing them with food, clothing and ongoing loving care.

That's the power of a shoebox gift – a gift that enabled a local church in the UK (who created it) and a local church in Swaziland (who distributed it) to touch the life of a child in need.

The Greatest Journey: Introducing Children to Jesus and the Christian Life

Many churches that give out Operation Christmas Child gift-filled shoeboxes will later invite the same children to take part in "The Greatest Journey." The Greatest Journey is a voluntary follow-up course to Operation Christmas Child. This twelve-lesson course introduces children to the gospel, helps them to develop a personal faith, and enables them to pray for and share the Good News of Jesus with their family and friends. Local church volunteers run the courses, having been trained and equipped with lesson plans and ideas for interaction. Memory verses, worship songs, illustrated Bible stories, quizzes and games all help children to stay engaged and learn.

Every child who completes the course is invited with their families to attend a Graduation Ceremony at which they receive a copy of the New Testament in their own language and a Graduation Certificate. This public recognition is all part of affirming them and helping them to understand how loved and valued they are by God. Please visit www.samaritans-purse.org.uk/the-greatest-journey to find out more. A gift of just £4 can enable a child overseas to participate in The Greatest Journey at a nearby church. Thank you.

TURN ON THE TAP, SAMARITAN'S PURSE

"Around 6,000 children die every day of waterborne illnesses."
(Source: UNICEF)

Every year 3.5 million people die of a waterborne illness due to dirty water; half of these are children. Around 6,000 children die every day – that's four children every minute! It doesn't have to be this way. Their deaths are preventable!

On average, people in Africa walk four miles a day to collect dirty water, often carrying weights of up to 20 kg. When families have to walk to find water, children miss out on school, and women and girls are vulnerable to attack. The dirty water is used for drinking, cooking and washing. When children then become sick, their parents need to stay at home and look after them. They are unable to go to work and earn their living.

Through Turn on the Tap, Samaritan's Purse has helped over one million people gain access to clean water and sanitation. We continue to work to improve the situation for people in countries like Liberia, Niger, Uganda, and Swaziland.

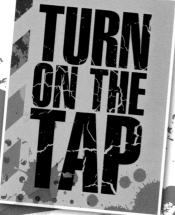

How We Help

Samaritan's Purse
INTERNATIONAL RELIEF

- *Water supplies:* Samaritan's Purse provides technical support to enable communities to access safe water through digging wells, drilling boreholes, capping springs and installing hand pumps. Where access to clean water is not feasible, we enable communities to make dirty water safe by providing BioSand Water Filtration (BSF) units.

  - *Sanitation:* We sanitise water and work with communities to build properly ventilated latrines; these prevent contamination of ground water, avoiding crop damage and spread of disease.

- *Hygiene:* Samaritan's Purse trains church committees to run community hygiene workshops which demonstrate the link between poor hygiene and disease, and show how the risks can be minimised through hand-washing, safe waste disposal and careful food preparation.

How You Can Help Us

For lots of fun ideas on how you can help to raise money through Turn on the Tap, which will in turn provide access to clean water overseas, please go to http://www.turnonthetap.org.uk/get-involved. Why not go on a Walk for Water, organise a fundraising barbecue, go to work in fancy dress, or hold a church service that educates your community on the need for access to clean water?

In the UK we take clean water for granted. Today, worldwide, one in eight people still don't have access to clean water (source: WHO/UNICEF).

Please support Turn on the Tap and help us to reduce the number of children dying through waterborne diseases. Thank you very much.

Photography by David Lund

TEARFUND AND DINNER4GOOD

When we put our heart and soul into something, we can't help but be transformed. For people in the local churches we partner with around the world, this is exactly what is happening.

tearfund

Meet Christine

Years of relentless drought meant a daily struggle for survival. When staple crops of cassava and peanuts all failed, Christine and her five children had nothing to eat, and nothing to sell for an income.

Photograph by Geoff Crawford / Tearfund

Ending poverty long term

Tearfund offers long-term solutions so that wherever we work, every child, mum, dad, grandpa and grandma can live life to the full. We offer training, education and support through local churches to release people from poverty, for good.

This helps communities to feed themselves and provides life-changing benefits such as clean water, access to education, business skills, freedom from disease and hope for the future.

For Christine, transformation really has come through the local church. Tearfund's partner, the Anglican Church of Uganda, helped set up a women's farming group to help the community to grow orange trees and to start a kitchen garden of onions, tomatoes, green beans and sweet potatoes.

Now Christine is chairwoman of the Women's Group, and membership has grown to over fifty. Christine knows her hope has been restored.

"I pray all the women's livelihoods will be uplifted. We all just need a little help to get started."

Why support Tearfund?

Tearfund is a Christian international development agency working to end poverty and restore dignity and hope in some of the world's poorest countries. As much as possible, Tearfund works through local churches because we know that whole-life transformation can only be found through Jesus.

Will you be part of the story?

Across the world, there are people like Christine who need you to be part of their story of transformation. Just £35 could provide one woman like Christine with 500g of vegetable seeds and four fruit trees, and £70 could pay for 250 market garden growing areas.
Your donation will make a real difference to people like Christine.

Please visit www.tearfund.org/dinner4good and help change the lives of people like Christine around the world.

HOW TO SHARE YOUR FAITH

For many people who are not yet Christian, you may be the only Christian they meet. How you act and live speaks volumes to them. Not all of us are called to be evangelists, but all of us have a part to play.

Some of us are called to pray – to pray for the seed to fall on good soil and to continue to pray that the seed doesn't become fruitless because of the worries of life (Mark 4:1–20).

Some of us are called to look after people, both in and outside the church, showing them unconditional love regardless of what is going on.

Some of us are called to be involved in social action projects, meeting the needs of our communities.

All of us are called to be the best we can be in whatever jobs we have, or where we live. We are all called to love others. It is this love that attracts people to us. It is essential that we continue to love people, even when there is no sign of them becoming Christian and also afterwards. We love people because we love them, not so that they will one day become Christians!

WHY SHARE YOUR FAITH?

Go therefore and make disciples of all the nations, baptizing them in the name of the Father and of the Son and of the Holy Spirit, teaching them to observe all things that I have commanded you; and lo, I am with you always, even to the end of the age. (Matthew 28:19–20)

The thief does not come except to steal, and to kill, and to destroy. I have come that they may have life, and that they may have it more abundantly. (John 10:10)

For God so loved the world that He gave His only begotten Son, that whoever believes in Him should not perish but have everlasting life. For God did not send His Son into the world to condemn the world, but that the world through Him might be saved. He who believes in Him is not condemned; but he who does not believe is condemned already, because he has not believed in the name of the only begotten Son of God. (John 3:16–18)

THE GEORGE VERWER STORY: PRAYER LEADS TO SALVATION

This story is reproduced with kind permission of George Verwer and is based on his website www.georgeverwer.com and the book Spiritual Revolution: The Story of OM by Ian Randall.

At the age of fourteen, George Verwer was given a Gospel of St John in his high school in Ramsey, New Jersey, and on the first page he signed a pledge promising to read it each day. He did this for three years before he was finally converted to the Lord. The Gospel was given to him by Dorothea Clapp, an elderly lady who had prayed for eighteen years for the students in that school – or, in George's own words, had put him "on her Holy Ghost hit list!" Mrs Clapp prayed that students would come to know Jesus in a personal way; and daringly asked God that they would be witnesses for Christ in many parts of the world. In 1955, aged sixteen, George Verwer made a personal commitment to Christ in Madison Square Garden, New York, at a rally organised by Jack Wyrtzen where Billy Graham was the speaker.

As President of the Ramsey High School student council, George gave out Gospels of St John in the school, and within a year, 200 of his fellow students had made a commitment to Christ.

Shortly after his conversion George said to God, "Only one thing I want in life – I want to learn to pray, to love you, I want to know you and I want to commune with you."

George Verwer is best known for founding Operation Mobilisation, a ministry of evangelism, discipleship training and church planting. Operation Mobilisation reaches across the world through the ministry of their ship *Logos Hope* and over 6,100 people working in over 110 nations to make Christ known to all they meet.

All of this began with the faithful prayer of Dorothea Clapp. I firmly believe (writes Rebekah) that if she had not prayed and had not given George a Gospel, he would not have accomplished all he has today.

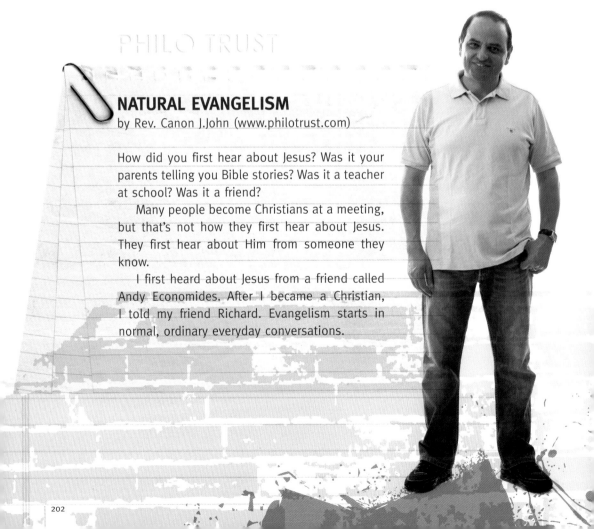

PHILO TRUST

NATURAL EVANGELISM
by Rev. Canon J.John (www.philotrust.com)

How did you first hear about Jesus? Was it your parents telling you Bible stories? Was it a teacher at school? Was it a friend?

Many people become Christians at a meeting, but that's not how they first hear about Jesus. They first hear about Him from someone they know.

I first heard about Jesus from a friend called Andy Economides. After I became a Christian, I told my friend Richard. Evangelism starts in normal, ordinary everyday conversations.

Jerusalem, Judea and Beyond

The evangelistic strategy given to us by Jesus is recorded in the opening chapter of Acts where Jesus said:

> You will receive power when the Holy Spirit comes on you; and you will be my witnesses in Jerusalem, and in all Judea and Samaria, and to the ends of the earth. (Acts 1:8 NIV)

The word "power" here means energy. Jesus promises us that the Holy Spirit will give us energy; and this is one of the greatest assurances we have: that despite our tiredness, the Holy Spirit empowers us to witness.

"Witnesses" are people who tell what they have seen and experienced to others. Then comes the bombshell: "Jerusalem … Judea … Samaria … and to the ends of the earth." Jesus is not talking about the disciples just witnessing over some cosy suppers with another dozen or so friends on the shores of Lake Galilee.

Why does Jesus instruct His disciples to start in Jerusalem? Because it was where they lived. We, too, need to share our faith where we are. There are three natural access areas:

1. Kinship – those with whom we share a common kinship, our family and our close friends
2. Community – the people we meet regularly: for example, the window cleaner, the newsagent and our neighbours
3. Common interest – those with whom we share the same meeting place at a gym or a club

Note what Jesus' instruction to one new believer was:

> Go home to your family and tell them how much the Lord has done for you. (Mark 5:19 NIV1984)

Some of you might be thinking, "If I go to my family and friends and tell them I'm a Christian, I'm going to feel awkward and embarrassed. They know what I'm like!"

Remember, we are a witness whether we want to be one or not. Either we are a good one or a poor one. You and I may be the only Bible people ever read.

The key is to be you. You could go to someone, or write or phone, saying, "It's just occurred to me that we have known each other for a long time, but I have never told you about the most important thing in my life. Besides, how can I really value you and not share the most important thing in my life?"

Sowing the Seed

No farmer ever suggested we should put fully grown plants into the ground in order to harvest their produce! Neither did Jesus suggest such a thing. We are only asked to sow seeds: a word, a kind action, and an ear that is truly sensitive to the felt need of someone hurting.

Our tendency is to focus on one person and be "over-generous" and try to sow a plant! Sadly, we often focus on one plant: we drown it in water, watch it like a hawk, and fertilise it like crazy with one Bible verse and one "holy experience" after another! Even though there is much more garden growing up around us, we are focused on one plant, one person.

Sometimes, when we have sown a seed in someone, we want them to become a Christian urgently and we get preoccupied with them (like a pregnancy!). But it may not be time for the birth.

Our responsibility is to sow seeds. It is God who will produce the crop. Later in the process, of course, we must be around so that God can say to us, "It's time for the harvest," or "Sow again," or "Fertilize a little," or "Cultivate with water." We cannot make the seeds grow or mature or ripen with fruit. We are the sowers and harvesters, and if we learn to do those things well, we won't get frustrated trying to produce fruit.

Some of the most natural evangelism we can do is to sow seeds of kindness and love to someone over a period of time. I once met a Christian couple; when asked how they evangelised, the husband looked embarrassed. He explained that he and his wife were not great speakers, but they tried to serve God by visiting an old people's home, to help people have their baths. He had no need to be embarrassed. This is a wonderful example of seed-growing, not plant-throwing! To do such as this is to share the fruits of the Spirit, and if we do this generously then "God is able to make all grace abound" (2 Corinthians 9:8 NIV1984). The promise is that as we share and sow our time, talents and resources with those who do not know Christ, then His grace will abound.

When the Seeds Begin to Grow

When the seeds begin to grow, people will begin to drop some telltale remark showing that they are interested in more. Have a listening ear to what they are really saying. They might say, "I remember when I used to go to Sunday school," or "I was married in church," or "I feel burnt out," or even, "Things have been difficult since my mum died."

Remember that God has appointed us to be "Christian information officers" – let's expect people to be interested! Don't be afraid to ask what someone believes and what involvement they already have had in the Christian faith. What do they think of it? Can you invite them to a Joyce Meyer conference or to a church service?

Also, be positive! We often say, in a voice which has admitted defeat before we have even got an answer, "I don't suppose you'd be free on Sunday evening to come to a special service at our church?" Or, "I know it's not really your scene, but you might find it interesting."

Instead, prayerfully expect people to be intrigued and interested! I remember a girl at her baptism; in her testimony she said, "My Christian friend built a bridge from her heart to mine, and Christ walked over it."

In a Nutshell

"I repeat what I told you once before when we feared we might be left without a radio station: God's best microphone is Christ, and Christ's best microphone is the church, and the church is all of us. Let each one of us, in our own job, in our own vocations – married or single people, bishop, priest, deacon, student, nurse, labourer – each one in our own place live in faith intensely and feel that in our surroundings we are a true microphone of God our Lord." (Oscar Romero)

Prayer:
Loving Father,
Lead us by Your Spirit to our faith in Christ.
May how we live speak of His Word to the world.
May what we say testify to our life in Him.
So that, as we know and love Him more, others may come to know and love Him too.
Amen.

SHARING FAITH WITH NEIGHBOURS
This article was based on an interview with Rev. Andy Economides

Inviting your Neighbours to Christian Events

"Society has changed so much that we live in ghettos and castles, not knowing people."

Over many years, I have built up relationships with my neighbours, having meals at Christmas, talking over the fence. It was deliberate, intentional, even when it was inconvenient to chat or I was having a bad time. This produced a nice community feeling. My neighbours knew from day one that I was a Christian. If they asked questions about my life and church work, I would answer, but I didn't speak directly about faith. Often my neighbours would come to the Christmas carol

service. I have been friends with some of my neighbours for twenty-six years! I often invited them to dinner, the pub or events.

A few years ago, I invited seventeen guests, including my immediate neighbours, to a dinner for 100 people in a hotel in Chichester. Eric Delve presented the gospel and gave people an opportunity to respond to Jesus, and some of my neighbours did respond. My neighbours knew what they were coming to and the invitation was based on friendship. I was able to invite seventeen people because I was confident that the speaker wouldn't let me down. It is the church's responsibility to put on high-quality events, to give confidence to church people that if they invite friends or neighbours it won't be boring, irrelevant or cheesy. If it's a good event, with good food included, people will come again.

If you invite a neighbour to a Christian event, it is essential to check with them how they found the evening, and be willing to answer any questions they may have. I held a follow-up group after the dinner in Chichester; one neighbour prayed the "prayer of salvation," but didn't feel comfortable sharing his thoughts in a group... We need to be flexible.

Don't be discouraged if people don't always respond to the gospel, as they may bear fruit later, and I believe that if people pray that they will be more effective in sharing their faith, God will answer their prayers. Just because you might not see results doesn't mean it isn't worth it. I believe every Christian can share their faith and see results.

Door to Door

As part of a survey about local community, we knocked on people's doors. On one occasion, whn I called back six months later to one of the houses, the couple remembered me from before and invited me in for a chat. I persuaded Lyndon and his wife Barbara to attend a dinner for 100 people where J.John was speaking. Lyndon, at the end of the dinner, said, "You Christians have something really special that I like."

I gave Lyndon a gospel book and told him to let me know if he prayed the prayer of salvation after reading it. He became a Christian the same night he read the book. Not long afterwards I was invited round to his house, and then every fortnight I would go round to his house for coffee and a chat; he had young children, meaning he couldn't leave the house. He later started attending church, became a church leader, went to theological college and became an Anglican minister. His wife also became a Christian and so did all their children.

Long-term Door Knocking

Over ten years, I systematically knocked on the doors of four streets; Swanfield Drive was one of them. I would take one or two people with me, to train them. Once or twice we would do a leaflet drop, but what worked best was knocking on the door and getting to know people over time; this way we could build long-term relationships. We would tell the people that we had spiritual responsibility for them and wanted to check how they were. I would often prayer-walk every street, just praying for families.

Our current church, Immanuel, in Chichester, knocks on doors offering to do DIY jobs, always refusing offers of payment. Praying for people and offering help creates opportunities. People often ask questions. Some people have come to church as a result.

> *"Many people stop because they are not seeing results; people don't do the long-term stuff any more. If people did things like this long term, I think we would all be amazed at the results."*

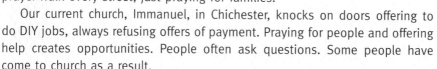

GOSSIPING THE GOSPEL TO YOUR NEIGHBOUR

by Rebekah Brettle

All of us have a story about how we became a Christian, or how God has helped us through a difficult period of our lives. Be ready to tell your story in a concise way, in case someone asks you. Sometimes an opportunity to share your story will come up naturally in conversation as you talk about your life or what happened at church.

If you are getting to know your neighbour well, it will become natural to talk about all aspects of your life. If God has done something amazing in your

church, for example if a healing has taken place, why would you not share this story? Your neighbour can decide for themselves if they believe you or not. Sharing your life story as opportunities arise should be natural. The power of your own stories of what God is doing in your life and in other people's lives should not be underestimated!

Don't be afraid to share moments of doubt or difficulties in your life and how God has helped you. The stories of our pain and how God helped us through are sometimes more powerful than stories of miracles.

LEADING YOUR NEIGHBOUR TO CHRIST

by Steve Mullins

In this section we will be looking briefly at how you help your neighbour to "cross the line," as it were, and commit their life to Christ. This can be the hardest but most rewarding part of evangelism, and it is most certainly the most important.

Let's just say you have now had several meetings and discussions with your neighbour about what it means to be a Christian and the difference Jesus has made in your life, but the big question, "When will they give their life to Jesus?" continues to nag at you. You ask yourself, "What else can I say? What more can I do?" "Our conversations have been going on for months but I've still not been able to close the deal," is the issue we will look at here, and possibly also the frustration you are now faced with.

Well firstly, don't get too caught up in the trap of getting stressed because a decision has not been made yet. You have been building a relationship with your friend or neighbour and that takes time. It is better to take time and see a proper decision made than to rush things, only for the seed that has been planted to wither away as quickly as it grew. Having said that, the gospel is an urgent matter. We need balance.

This next point may be obvious, but it needs saying anyway: If you are seeking to lead someone to Christ, the whole process must be bathed in prayer. That is part of the responsibility God gives us in our evangelism. Someone once said, "I need to talk to God about the people before I talk to the people about God." Prayer is key in our evangelistic efforts.

For the sake of this article, I will give you the benefit of the doubt and assume that you have been praying conscientiously for your friend or neighbour throughout the time you have been talking with them. In terms of them making a decision for Christ, the prayer has changed from "Lord, give me an opportunity to talk to So-and-so about You," to "Lord, thank You for giving me the opportunities to talk to So-and-so for the past few months, but Father, give me the boldness to now lead them to You and see them make a commitment to You."

There are two possible options in terms of you leading the person to Christ. The first option would be the dream scenario – where your friend says to you, "So how do I become a Christian?" The second option is a bit harder and would involve you taking the plunge at the appropriate moment and saying something like, "We've been chatting for a few months now, we've talked about various issues surrounding Christianity, and I've shared my story with you about what Jesus means to me – but what about you? What's stopping you becoming a Christian?" This is not a question designed to accuse them but rather to allow them to honestly respond; it can be asked in a gentle, sincere manner as you both sit in the sunny conservatory drinking your freshly made cappuccino!

One thing to note here: many times in our conversations with people, there is a tendency for them to throw in "red herrings" to try and move the conversation on to other issues or people, such as asking, "What about all those people who have never heard about Jesus?" The way to deal with this is to keep focused on the person you are talking with. You can normally tell if this is a question that genuinely worries them or a question just to throw you off track. Hopefully, over the time you have been talking with them, any key issues, concerns or problems they have will have been dealt with, and so now they are either ready to ask you, or ready for you to ask them, about giving their life to Jesus. The key thing for you to remember is: stay focused on them.

So back to what happens next. The key question has been put. There are no barriers in the way – your friend has replied, "Nothing, really," when asked the question about what's stopping them giving their life to Christ, and he or she has stated that they are ready to make a commitment to Christ.

This is it – the moment you have been waiting for and praying for. So what happens next?

There are several things that you will need to make clear just to help avoid any confusion. Of course when anyone comes to Christ what they are doing is not fully understood. It is a step of faith. However, as they take this step it is useful to emphasise to them that they are not joining a church or a religion; rather they are surrendering their life to the living Lord Jesus Christ.

Before praying any kind of "prayer of salvation" with them, it is useful to just briefly go over the gospel again. It is good to have a number of what I call "salvation verses" memorised or, even better, to have a Bible handy and get the person to read out the verses for themselves.

Below are just a few verses that I believe are key in leading someone to Christ (all the verses are taken from the New King James Version of the Bible).

1. They need to understand God loves them:

> For God so loved the world that He gave His only begotten Son, that whoever believes in Him should not perish but have everlasting life. (John 3:16)

2. They need to recognise they are separated from God by their sin:

> But your iniquities have separated you from your God;
> And your sins have hidden His face from you.
> (Isaiah 59:2)

> For all have sinned and fall short of the glory of God.
> (Romans 3:23)

3. They need to see that God has made a way for sin to be dealt with and for us to come into relationship with Him:

> But God demonstrates His own love toward us, in that while we were still sinners, Christ died for us.
> (Romans 5:8)

4. They need to see that God offers them an invitation and it is an invitation to a new and eternal life:

> But as many as received Him, to them He gave the right to become children of God, to those who believe in His name.
> (John 1:12)

> Therefore, if anyone is in Christ, he is a new creation; old things have passed away; behold, all things have become new.
> (2 Corinthians 5:17)

There are obviously many other Bible verses that can be used, so you can find others for yourself. However, it is good to just run over this brief gospel outline with your friend.

Basically they are doing four things:

1. Recognising that they are a sinner, that they have a spiritual need
2. Repenting – that is turning away from all that they know to be wrong
3. Believing that Jesus Christ died for them on the cross
4. Receiving through prayer, the Lord Jesus Christ into their life.

It is a good idea, while going through these steps, to allow your friend to ask any questions or make any comments. We need to talk in simple terms and use language they will understand (stay away from too much Biblical jargon, such as "You need to be washed in the blood of the Lamb, brother"), but at the same time we must not dilute the truth of the gospel.

Also, although I have given an outline here, we must always be led by the Holy Spirit and be listening to Him as we are sharing the gospel and seeking to bring people to Christ.

Once you have gone through these steps with your friend, you can lead them in a prayer. Here is just an example of what you could pray:

> Dear Lord Jesus Christ, I come to You now, recognising that I am not perfect but a sinner.
> I confess my sin to You now and thank You for dying for me.
> On the basis of Your promises I thank You that You are faithful and fair and will forgive my sin.
> I put my trust in You now and ask You to come into my life by the power of Your Spirit and make me new. Empower me to turn from all that I know to be wrong.
> I receive Your love, peace, and forgiveness now, and thank You for the gift of eternal life that I now receive.
> Amen.

That's it – but not quite!

That's just the first step in your friend's new journey with God. He or she may say, "I don't feel any different," but you can assure them that is normal. What they have done is taken a step of faith to trust and believe in a God who loves and cares for them.

Your job is not finished here though. You now need to encourage them to read the Bible; suggest they start reading through Luke's or Mark's Gospel. Maybe you could buy them a Bible or have already done so. They also need to learn to pray, tell someone else what they have done in becoming a Christian, and start to meet with other Christians – all things you can help them with.

Leading someone to Christ is exciting, especially if you have got to know them quite well and can have further input into getting them started in their walk with God. May you know God's blessing and power as you seek to share your faith with your neighbour and lead them into a relationship with the living Lord Jesus Christ.

"GOD ONLY HAS YOU NOW – BUT THAT IS ALL HE NEEDS!"

by Mark Oakes, UK Director – Christ for all Nations (the ministry of evangelists Reinhard Bonnke and Daniel Kolenda)

The title for this article is a quote from evangelist Reinhard Bonnke. How does it resonate with you? We face a mighty challenge of faith when we look at that statement in the context of sharing our faith and seeing the miraculous in our lives. Of course God can do much without us, but His grace is such that He chooses to use ordinary people like me and you to carry out His wonderful works on the earth!

Over the centuries, many passionate men and women of faith have lived lives of surrender and obedience to the call of the great commission (Matthew 28:18–20). They laid down everything to tell others about an amazing God who changes lives. They truly understood what the "Go" of the great commission means and applied it to their feet as well!

I've been studying one man in particular who was so ordinary, yet when he made that connection into the realm of the impossible through faith, he became one of the most extraordinary characters you could think of! I'm talking about a man called Smith Wigglesworth.

Smith was often referred to as an "apostle of faith" and was a great pioneer of the Pentecostal revival that occurred a century ago. Many thousands of people came to faith through his preaching of the gospel, and many were healed of incurable illness and disease.

The year 1859 marked his birth into a poor family in rural Bradford. He grew up in tough conditions, both practically and spiritually, as neither of his parents had any belief in God. Yet even as a boy Smith had an understanding of God and would also talk to Him in prayer. His grandmother was a believer, however, and Smith would regularly attend church with her. He became a Christian before his teenage years and knew and understood then that he would be a "soul-winner" for the rest of his life. In fact, we are told, the very first person he "won for Christ" was his own dear mother!

Smith was noted to be a man who could not speak well or communicate effectively in his younger years. Due to being tall, he was able to get a job at the age of nine in the milling industry, as an education was not deemed to be important then. He had not learned to read or write.

But by the time Smith was twenty years of age he had led hundreds of people to Christ! Every week he would gather ragged, dirty, barefooted girls and boys around him. He fed them not only physical food, bought with his hard-earned money, but also satisfied the spiritual hunger they faced.

This man was no different from you or me! Sure, things would have looked very different over a hundred years ago. However, we know that "Jesus Christ is the same, yesterday, today and forever" (Hebrews 13:8). He exists across, time, culture, space, style and a million and one other things.

Smith understood that the same power available to you and me today was there and available to him – he took it, applied it, and saw God work.

Let me quote Wigglesworth:

> The Lord wants all saved people to receive power from on High – power to witness, power to act, power to live, and power to show forth the divine manifestation of God within. The power of God will take you out of your own plans and put you into the plan of God.

Do you understand the power available to you today? Why you need it? What impact this power could have in your life and the effect it could have on all around you?

You need to read the whole of Acts chapter 2. Understand that the church was born in the fire! I love the contrast between the start and end of this chapter. The beginning outlines how the fire of God descended, how each person was filled with the Holy Spirit and how they began to speak in other tongues. Can you imagine it all?

The end of the chapter finishes with what I would describe as the outcome: the reason why they were baptised with fire and the Holy Ghost! We read that they devoted themselves to teaching, fellowship, the breaking of bread and to prayer. They were all filled with awe, and many signs and wonders were done by the apostles. They were together. They had everything in common. They sold their possessions and gave to the poor and those in need. They broke bread, ate together, praised God and enjoyed the favour of all people.

Then for me comes such a great verse: "And the Lord added to their number daily those who were being saved" (Acts 2:47 NIV). Oh, how I wish I could have seen all this! Yet that same Holy Spirit is available to you and me today and will work through us in the same way, if we would be open and willing to receive Him.

Two other things inspire me about Wigglesworth as I head to the conclusion now.

First, a story I read of him being at a church where there was a "Holy Spirit baptism" type of meeting happening that night. It tells of a married couple of whom the wife was seeking the baptism in that meeting, but she received absolutely nothing. At the end of the night the couple approached Smith to say that the wife so desired the baptism and would he go back to their house to continue in prayer?

Smith accepted the invitation and, following the meeting, went home with them. The woman set about producing cups of tea and sandwiches, but an impatient Smith pulled her and the husband to their knees on the floor, exclaiming that he had not come for niceties but to truly seek God for what she desired.

He was recorded as saying that after much prayer and toil in seeking God, the wife received the baptism of the Holy Spirit at 3.00 a.m. that morning.

This whole thing speaks to me of perseverance. The Holy Spirit is a wind – we can't always be confined by our expectations of when and how we will receive the baptism. We have to be in the right time and place. We should always be seeking Him and be prepared to go the extra mile, whatever the cost.

Many leave from our churches at the end of a meeting, disappointed that in the five minutes of an often impassioned altar-call, when God is given a few moments to work and hands are laid on by less than expectant people, they have received nothing. "Oh, to persevere and see the establishment and fruit of all that God wants to do in your life!" said Smith.

The second point is a little shorter. Smith made a deal with God that he would not put his head down on his pillow each night until he had "won someone for Christ." It proved to be very fruitful!

I worked out that if my church all took this on board and made that kind of deal with God, we would see 146,000 people saved in a year! That is without the multiplication effect of new believers being added into it.

This begs the question: How passionate are we about sharing our faith?

Now, Smith Wigglesworth is no longer walking these shores. He's healing no one. He's leading no one personally to Christ. The meetings have gone. The churches have evolved into memorials of the things that were once great there.

God no longer has Wigglesworth nor other great men and women of God left here. All He has is you.

What will you do with the call of His voice upon your life?

Listen carefully and apply prayerfully:

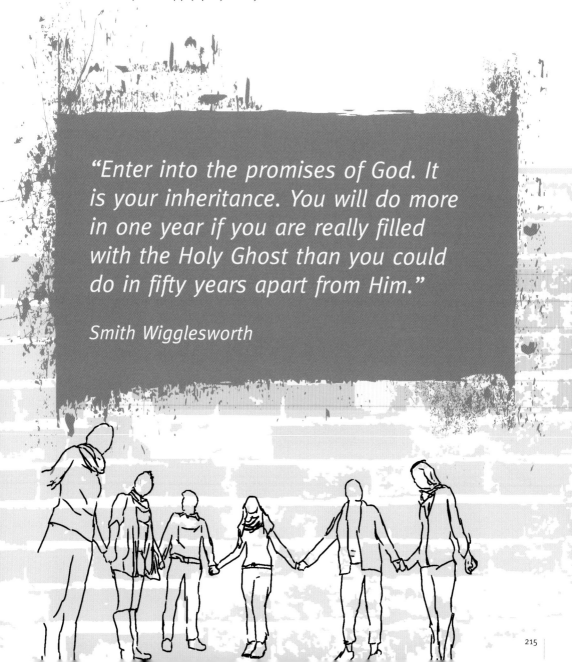

"Enter into the promises of God. It is your inheritance. You will do more in one year if you are really filled with the Holy Ghost than you could do in fifty years apart from Him."

Smith Wigglesworth

EVANGELISM RESOURCES

LOOKINGFORGOD.COM
by Dave Lucas

LookingforGod.com is an evangelistic website owned and run by United Christian Broadcasters (UCB) that aims to introduce people to Jesus through the internet. Furthermore, we aim to encourage new Christians to attend a church to help them become active members of the Christian faith. Throughout 2011, almost 40,000 people visited the website and 1,500 people became Christians.

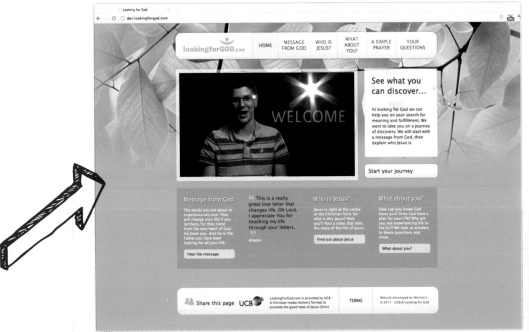

In the latter half of 2011, a new website was launched which is allowing people to interact with the site in a better way and for more people to become Christians. We are on target to see more than 2,000 people become Christians through the website in 2012. Please feel free to visit the site, where I hope you will gain a firsthand understanding of our vision, values and aims: www.lookingforGod.com.

Looking for God are asking for people to help with our online mentoring system, where local churches will take on the role of mentoring new Christians and seekers from their area in an online environment. The aim is to create a successful dialogue that encourages people to attend a church to further their understanding of Jesus and faith. We are looking for churches to partner with us that may be able to spend some time working with people who are searching or have recently made a commitment. Would you be interested in helping us with this vision? Please get in touch with us.

LookingforGod.com is also looking for churches to be part of our database for our online Church Directory. Any user will be able to search for a local church near to them throughout the UK and Republic of Ireland, so allow them to search for your church too! We are looking for more than 1,200 churches to be part of this database, and your church could help people find a place where they can learn about God through the church environment. Would you be interested in your church joining this network? Please feel free to get in touch with us.

You may also be interested in some printable resources that you can download from the UCB website. These include posters, postcards and business cards that can advertise Looking for God and encourage people to search for the gospel. Please visit www.ucb.co.uk/lfgresources for more information.

Finally, Looking for God is interested in visiting your church to speak to the congregation and church leadership about the Looking for God project and UCB in general. If you would be interested in having us visit you, please get in touch with us.

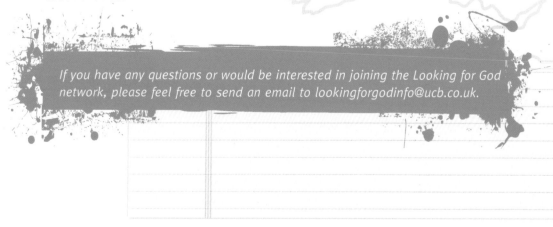

If you have any questions or would be interested in joining the Looking for God network, please feel free to send an email to lookingforgodinfo@ucb.co.uk.

Wendy Thomas

FATHER'S LOVE LETTER

Pray for Scotland, Street Pastors, Neighbourhood Prayer Network and Urban Saints are hoping that churches will deliver the Father's Love Letter to as many people as possible around Valentine's Day or Father's Day or at other times of the year. Please see page 220.

We want to highlight two projects where this resource has been used positively to share the gospel. The following article is written by Wendy Thomas (Street Pastors National Prayer Co-ordinator).

The cry of a Father's heart from Genesis to Revelation...

Father's Love Letter

My Child...

You may not know me,
but I know everything about you...Psalm 139:1
I know when you sit down and when you rise up...Psalm 139:2
I am familiar with all your ways ...Psalm 139:3   Even the very hairs on your head are numbered...Matthew 10:29-31
For you were made in my image...Genesis 1:27   In me you live and move and have your being...Acts 17:28   For you
are my offspring...Acts 17:28   I knew you even before you were conceived...Jeremiah 1:4-5   I chose you when I
planned creation...Ephesians 1:11-12   You were not a mistake...Psalm 139:15-16   For all your days are written in my book
...Psalm 139:15-16   I determined the exact time of your birth and where you would live...Acts 17:26   You are fearfully
and wonderfully made...Psalm 139:14   I knit you together in your mother's womb...Psalm 139:13   And brought you
forth on the day you were born ...Psalm 71:6   I have been misrepresented by those who don't know me...John 8:41-44
I am not distant and angry, but am the complete expression of love...1 John 4:16   And it is my desire to lavish
my love on you...1 John 3:1   Simply because you are my child and I am your Father...1 John 3:1   I offer you more
than your earthly father ever could...Matthew 7:11   For I am the perfect Father...Matthew 5:48   Every good gift that you
receive comes from my hand...James 1:17   For I am your provider and I meet all your needs...Matthew 6:31-33
My plan for your future has always been filled with hope...Jeremiah 29:11   Because I love you with an everlasting
love...Jeremiah 31:3   My thoughts toward you are countless as the sand on the seashore...Psalm 139:17-18   And I rejoice
over you with singing...Zephaniah 3:17   I will never stop doing good to you...Jeremiah 32:40   For you are my treasured
possession...Exodus 19:5   I desire to establish you with all my heart and all my soul...Jeremiah 32:41   And I want to
show you great and marvelous things...Jeremiah 33:3   If you seek me with all your heart, you will find me
...Deuteronomy 4:29   Delight in me and I will give you the desires of your heart ...Psalm 37:4   For it is I who gave you
those desires...Philippians 2:13   I am able to do more for you than you could possibly imagine...Ephesians 3:20   For I am
your greatest encourager....2 Thessalonians 2:16-17   I am also the Father who comforts you in all your troubles
...2 Corinthians 1:3-4   When you are brokenhearted, I am close to you...Psalm 34:18   As a shepherd carries a lamb, I have
carried you close to my heart...Isaiah 40:11   One day I will wipe away every tear from your eyes...Revelation 21:3-4
And I'll take away all the pain you have suffered on this earth...Revelation 21:4   I am your Father and I love you
even as I love my son, Jesus...John 17:23   For in Jesus my love for you is revealed ...John 17:26   He is the exact
representation of my being...Hebrews 1:3   And He came to demonstrate that I am for you, not against you
...Romans 8:31   And to tell you that I am not counting your sins...2 Corinthians 5:18-19   Jesus died so that you and I
could be reconciled...2 Corinthians 5:18-19   His death was the ultimate expression of my love for you...1 John 4:10
I gave up everything I loved that I might gain your love...Romans 8:32   If you receive the gift of my son Jesus,
you receive me...1 John 2:23   And nothing will ever separate you from my love again...Romans 8:38-39   Come home and
I'll throw the biggest party heaven has ever seen...Luke 15:7   I have always been Father and will always be
Father...Ephesians 3:14-15   My question is...Will you be my child?...John 1:12-13   I am waiting for you...Luke 15:11-32

...Love, Your Dad
Almighty God

What Is the Father's Love Letter?

You can see a copy of the Father's Love Letter on the previous page. It is a collection of verses from Genesis to Revelation that tells the tale of God the Father's love for you, His child. Barry Adams, a Canadian minister, wrote it as a sermon illustration. He says:

> I can remember the day that I asked God to help me better comprehend His love in light of all the scriptures that I was now seeing throughout the Bible. In my heart, I immediately heard a still small voice say, "If you put the scriptures in the right order, they will form a love letter." That was in December 1998 and by January 1999 I had compiled a series of paraphrased scriptures into a PowerPoint presentation accompanied by Brian Doerksen's song "Faithful Father" that I played as a sermon illustration in my home church.
>
> I was amazed at how the congregation began to respond to this simple message of Father's love. Many of the people seemed to be having an intimate, powerful encounter with their Heavenly Father. Everywhere I played this simple presentation, the results were the same. I began to see, in a deeper way, the incredible need that we all have to be loved in a way that only God the Father can love us. It was at that point that I felt I needed to get this message on the internet. By November 1999, we launched www.FathersLoveLetter.com, offering the Father's Love Letter as a free Flash video.

The Story of Southend

In Southend-on-Sea in 2005 around Valentine's Day, the churches together delivered the Father's Love Letter to every home in the town (75,000 homes).

In Southend, the words of the Father's Love Letter were put inside a card, along with a response card that people could send off for a Christian magazine and an invitation to find out more about the Christian faith. The recipient was then able to opt for contact with a local church or a Christian. The Father's Love Letter was put into envelopes by hand by members of different churches across town and was delivered by hand to all the homes by Christians from various churches and denominations working together. As each letter was delivered, the volunteeers were praying, so all the streets in the town were prayer-walked as well. Over 300 people became Christians or came back to God, and there were many other stories of the impact this had.

People are still remembering the card today and it still affects them in a positive way. Could you do this in your town? It requires churches to work together to cover a wide geographical area. It can make a huge difference to people's lives and it is well worth it.

Pray for Scotland by Jean Black

I first discovered the Father's Love Letter compilation of scriptures in 2006. It was compiled in Canada by Barry Adams. At that time, we were preparing to have a fifty-day prayer journey driving and walking in every part of the nation of Scotland in 2007. In a DVD one of our leaders said our aim for the journey was to take the Father's love to every part of the nation. We felt that this piece of literature aided, in words, our desire to pray and speak this message. We added a prayer to the leaflet to help people make a personal response to God.

There is a population of 5 million in our nation of Scotland. We initially printed 250,000 leaflets, but the demand for them continues to this day. Last year we printed a further 10,000, this year 20,000. Most weeks we have a request for them. Every home in the Shetland Isles has received a copy. This year a minister on the island of Uist wanted to visit every home with the leaflets. A lady in Broughty Ferry, who works as a street pastor in the centre of Dundee, is also distributing them. On the streets of our cities they are being used as a tool for evangelism. They are also being used in many other places such as Healing Rooms and homes for the elderly, and there are two ministries which specifically teach seminars on the Father's transforming love.

Our prayer is for our broken society, for people to come into relationship with the Lord and intimacy with Him.

The Future...

Wouldn't it be wonderful if everyone in the UK received the Father's Love Letter? A coalition of Neighbourhood Prayer Network, Pray for Scotland, Street Pastors, Urban Saints and Love Your Streets are hoping that people and churches from all over the country will deliver the Father's Love Letter, so that everyone in the UK will receive a copy.

We are suggesting that the best way to give these out would be as a card, probably around Valentine's Day or Father's Day, or around the time of an Alpha course beginning. We suggest that, on the back of the card, you might want to have contact details for your church, or suggest that people contact UCB's Prayerline or Looking for God if they want to make a commitment to Christ.

We are working to produce some cards with this information on the back that should soon be available from our website (www.neighbourhoodprayer.net), subject to demand.

Wendy Thomas (Street Pastors) and Neighbourhood Prayer Network are also proposing that it might be an opportunity to invite people to a dinner, to explain the Father's love in more detail. This idea is only a suggestion.

ALPHA

Over three million people have been on an Alpha course (source: Christian Research). The ten-week course – revolving around food, a talk and a discussion afterwards – is still changing lives today. Neighbourhood Prayer Network loves Alpha and any similar initiatives. We are suggesting that people might eventually want to start inviting their neighbours to Alpha around September of the year. Here is an encouraging story to show how Alpha can transform a life of crime into one of hope.

Alpha

My Story by Darrell Tunningley

A convicted armed robber, drug dealer, addict and all-round nasty piece of work serving five and a half years is not your normal candidate to invite to an Alpha course! But that was me...

Written off by everyone, including myself. Growing up in Yorkshire in a "ruff" area, on a "ruff" estate, was never going to be the best start in life. Combine that with my own bad decisions and a strange desire to self-destruct and you have the perfect recipe for disaster.

So when a little muppet of a fella approached me in the prison workshop with an invite to Alpha, my first reaction was to slap him! The only reason I didn't was the offer of free coffee, biscuits and a chance to miss a little cell-time.

When I came to find it was being run by two retired nuns and a vicar, I almost bolted for the door! What could they possibly know about life?

For the first couple of weeks we gave them so much stick, but they just kept coming back at us with love and compassion. That made me stop, and I made the decision that they deserved a little bit more respect. I sort of said to myself, "Right, Darrell, for once in your life just shut up and listen to what someone else has got to say."

They were saying that the whole point wasn't just a clean slate. It was smashing up your old slate completely and getting a new one, a complete fresh start, being forgiven.

They said, "God loves you exactly as you are, but He loves you too much to leave you that way. He wants to take the best of who you are and get rid of the worst of who you are."

And it just made sense to me. Something clicked.

Because of that invitation, allowing Alpha to be used as the turning point, everything changed. Darrell Tunningley is now an Assemblies of God minister and part of the senior leadership of Hope Corner Community Church in the North-West of England, as well as an evangelist and equipper of churches. He is also the author of the best-selling book *Unreachable*.

He has dedicated his life to sharing the love of Christ in his community and around the world, by bringing hope to the lost.

Darrell is married to Rebekah and has two children, Benjamin and Lydia-Grace.

THE BOOK OF HOPE

by Jim Cronin (UCB)

Since 1987, an organisation called "OneHope" (formerly Book of Hope) has touched the lives of over 800 million children and young people, worldwide. Through printed materials, film, and increasingly using online digital resources, OneHope's goal is simple: "God's Word, every child."

Their story is a remarkable one, starting in civil-war torn El Salvador, where OneHope presented a simple children's Scripture book, called *The Book of Hope*, to every child in the nation. Now operating in eighty-five countries around the world, they project to reach an estimated 91.8 million children and young people in 2012.

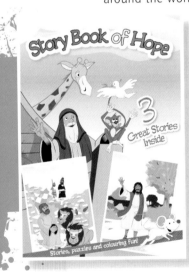

Here in the UK, OneHope has distributed over 4.4 million copies of *The Book of Hope*, 3 million in partnership with UCB, who teamed up with OneHope in 2007 to reach even more children. Now offering books and films for every age range from three to over eighteens, UCB and OneHope continue to work together in strategic partnership to create new ways to reach young people and partner with new ministries.

"I love it. It helps my kid get interested to read about the Bible. She loves reading the Bible now more than before, thanks to Books of Hope." (Testimony sent to UCB in May 2011).

So What Does a Book of Hope Look Like?

There are several versions of *The Book of Hope* in the UK, each designed to be ideal for a different age group, and all of them completely based on the Word of God. Whether it's a three-year-old's book with colouring-in pages, or an eighteen-year-old's book that has articles on how to make important life decisions, Scripture is at the centre, with activities to help to bring the message home. It's the Bible, applied.

Especially popular are the "Bags of Hope," which contain a *Book of Hope* and a daily devotional, and are perfect for Halloween (what's better than to give trick-or-treaters the Word of God!) and for Easter outreach. Why not order some for your group or church today, at www.bookofhope.co.uk.

ALTERNATIVE HALLOWEEN: PARTY IDEAS FROM SAMARITAN'S PURSE

Here in the UK, thousands of churches have discovered that shoeboxes open doors. They open doors for the church to connect with the community. They open doors for the church to show love in action. They open doors into hearts as people discover more about a loving God and His Son, Jesus Christ.

One of the ways that your local church could use Operation Christmas Child (see page 194 for details) as a mission tool at home is to throw a shoebox-packing party, or an Alternative Halloween Party. Why not try one of the following ideas...

Theme: "Treat a Child Overseas": Ask each child to bring an empty shoebox, some wrapping paper and some gifts for packing into their shoebox. See www.operationchristmaschild.org.uk

Fancy Dress: On your party invitation, list the countries that Samaritan's Purse send shoeboxes to and encourage all the young people to pick a country, research the flag, and come dressed in the colours of the flag (or in traditional dress for that country).

Story Cards: Make cards for each young person, containing the name and story of one child from overseas who has received a shoebox. See www.operationchristmaschild.org.uk.

Game: Pass the Shoebox – Instead of Pass the Parcel, how about getting one shoebox and filling it with various dares for each child to do? Play the music, and every time the music stops, the child holding the shoebox has to take out a piece of paper and complete the dare.

Game: Shoebox Treasure Hunt – Buy non-perishable covered sweets (check that no child has allergies) and hide them around the room. Divide the children into groups and then send them out to try to find the treasure and fill a shoebox with them. The shoebox with the most sweets wins.

DIARY OF THE YEAR
— MENU OF IDEAS
(For more ideas, please visit www.hopetogether.org.uk)

Adopt a Street and Prayer for Scotland's Lighthouses of Prayer run continuously throughout the year. This diary is a suggestion of activity over a year in your street. It refers to articles and resources mentioned earlier in this guide. It is designed so you can refer to each month individually.

CALENDAR

JANUARY

Prayer
We have the following prayer guides that you may find useful:

- **Neighbour Fridays:** This is found in the UCB resource *Prayer for Today*, where Neighbourhood Prayer Network writes the prayers for every Friday. There is a short prayer every Friday and a prayer challenge for your street. See page 170 for details.

- **Neighbourhood Prayer Triplets:** We are encouraging as many people as possible to form prayer triplets. This is a twelve-week guide that also aims to teach, in most cases letting Scripture speak for itself. We hope that prayer triplets will continue longer term and that this guide will give people confidence to pray. Please see page 98.

- **Neighbourhood Prayer Diary:** This is a weekly prayer diary produced in partnership with Tearfund. Each day has a theme with a list of people to pray for that day. See page 153.

CALENDAR

FEBRUARY

Prayer

We have the following prayer guides that you may find useful:

- **Neighbour Fridays:** This is found in the UCB resource *Prayer for Today*, where Neighbourhood Prayer Network writes the prayers for every Friday. There is a short prayer every Friday and a prayer challenge for your street. See page 170 for details.

- **Neighbourhood Prayer Triplets:** We are encouraging as many people as possible to form prayer triplets. This is a twelve-week guide that also aims to teach, in most cases letting Scripture speak for itself. We hope that prayer triplets will continue longer term and that this guide will give people confidence to pray. Please see page 98.

- **Neighbourhood Prayer Diary:** This is a weekly prayer diary produced in partnership with Tearfund. Each day has a theme with a list of people to pray for that day. See page 153.

- **Forty Days of Prayer:** This is designed to cover the Lent period and has a scripture, suggested prayers and a prayer challenge for this period. Additional versions will appear from time to time on the website.

Care

- **Do1nicething:** This is an initiative of Love Your Streets. Every day there is a suggestion of something that you can do during the forty days of Lent. Please visit www.do1nicething.org for details, and please if you use Twitter, tweet the correct tweet for the day and use #do1nicething.

CALENDAR

MARCH

Prayer

We have the following prayer guides that you may find useful:

- **Neighbour Fridays:** This is found in the UCB resource *Prayer for Today*; where Neighbourhood Prayer Network writes the prayers for every Friday. There is a short prayer every Friday and a prayer challenge for your street. See page 170 for details.

- **Neighbourhood Prayer Triplets:** We are encouraging as many people as possible to form prayer triplets. This is a twelve-week guide that also aims to teach, in most cases letting Scripture speak for itself. We hope that prayer triplets will continue longer term and that this guide will give people confidence to pray. Please see page 98.

- **Neighbourhood Prayer Diary:** This is a weekly prayer diary produced in partnership with Tearfund. Each day has a theme with a list of people to pray for that day. See page 153.

- **Forty Days of Prayer:** This is designed to cover the Lent period and has a scripture, suggested prayers and a prayer challenge for this period. Additional versions will appear from time to time on the website.

- **Festival of Life**

Care

- **Do1nicething:** This is an initiative of Love Your Streets. Every day there is a suggestion of something that you can do during the forty days of Lent. Please visit www.do1nicething.org for details and please, if you use Twitter, tweet the correct tweet for the day and use #do1nicething.

Share

- **The Book of Hope:** See article on page 222.

CALENDAR

APRIL

Prayer

We have the following prayer guides that you may find useful:

- **Neighbour Fridays:** This is found in the UCB resource *Prayer for Today*; where Neighbourhood Prayer Network writes the prayers for every Friday. There is a short prayer every Friday and a prayer challenge for your street. See page 170 for details.

- **Neighbourhood Prayer Triplets:** We are encouraging as many people as possible to form prayer triplets. This is a twelve-week guide that also aims to teach, in most cases letting Scripture speak for itself. We hope that prayer triplets will continue longer term and that this guide will give people confidence to pray. Please see page 98.

- **Neighbourhood Prayer Diary:** This is a weekly prayer diary produced in partnership with Tearfund. Each day has a theme with a list of people to pray for that day. See page 153.

- **Forty Days of Prayer:** This is designed to cover the Lent period and has a scripture, suggested prayers and a prayer challenge for this period. Additional versions will appear from time to time on the website.

Care

- **Do1nicething:** This is an initiative of Love Your Streets. Every day there is a suggestion of something that you can do during the forty days of Lent. Please visit www.do1nicething.org for details and please, if you use Twitter, tweet the correct tweet for the day and use the #do1nicething.

- **Give out Easter Cards:** Can you give out Easter cards to your neighbours?

April continued...

Share

- **Newspapers/Church Magazine:** See page 81 for the article "Real News." Could your church organise people to give out a newspaper to your local community, sharing the gospel in a contemporary way?

- **Invitation of Neighbours to Easter Services:** Either personally, if you know your neighbours well, or through a church leaflet.

- **Prayer Request Cards:** Please see page 169. We are suggesting churches or home groups might want to post or give out prayer request cards to their neighbours, asking your neighbours what you would like them to pray for over the next two weeks. There is usually an address to return the card to – perhaps a church – or they can be collected individually. This is often an opportunity to get to know your neighbours, though few people like to do this on the street they live on, choosing to work on another street. This activity is not suitable for children.

Prayer

We have the following prayer guides that you may find useful:

- **Neighbour Fridays:** This is found in the UCB resource *Prayer for Today*, where Neighbourhood Prayer Network writes the prayers for every Friday. There is a short prayer every Friday and a prayer challenge for your street. See page 170 for details.

- **Neighbourhood Prayer Triplets:** We are encouraging as many people as possible to form prayer triplets. This is a twelve-week guide that also aims to teach, in most cases letting Scripture speak for itself. We hope that prayer triplets will continue longer term and that this guide will give people confidence to pray. Please see page 98.

- **Neighbourhood Prayer Diary:** This is a weekly prayer diary produced in partnership with Tearfund. Each day has a theme with a list of people to pray for that day. See page 153.

Care and Share

- **Pentecost Celebrations**

CALENDAR

JUNE

Prayer

We have the following prayer guides that you may find useful:

- **Neighbour Fridays:** This is found in the UCB resource *Prayer for Today*, where Neighbourhood Prayer Network writes the prayers for every Friday. There is a short prayer every Friday and a prayer challenge for your street. See page 170 for details.

- **Neighbourhood Prayer Triplets:** We are encouraging as many people as possible to form prayer triplets. This is a twelve-week guide that also aims to teach, in most cases letting Scripture speak for itself. We hope that prayer triplets will continue longer term and that this guide will give people confidence to pray. Please see page 98.

- **Neighbourhood Prayer Diary:** This is a weekly prayer diary produced in partnership with Tearfund. Each day has a theme with a list of people to pray for that day. See page 153.

- **Prayer Walking:** Please see prayer-walking guide on page 162.

Care and Share

- **Pentecost Celebrations**

- **The Big Lunch:** Invite your neighbours to The Big Lunch. This is a secular project run by the Eden Project, usually held at the beginning of every June. The idea is to get as many people in the UK to have lunch once a year with their neighbours. Please visit www.thebiglunch. com for details.

CALENDAR

JULY

Prayer

We have the following prayer guides that you may find useful:

- **Neighbour Fridays:** This is found in the UCB resource *Prayer for Today*, where Neighbourhood Prayer Network writes the prayers for every Friday. There is a short prayer every Friday and a prayer challenge for your street. See page 170 for details.

- **Neighbourhood Prayer Triplets:** We are encouraging as many people as possible to form prayer triplets. This is a twelve-week guide that also aims to teach, in most cases letting Scripture speak for itself. We hope that prayer triplets will continue longer term and that this guide will give people confidence to pray. Please see page 98.

- **Neighbourhood Prayer Diary:** This is a weekly prayer diary produced in partnership with Tearfund. Each day has a theme with a list of people to pray for that day. See page 153.

- **Prayer Walking:** Please see prayer-walking guide on page 162.

Care and Share

- **Summer Church Barbecue**
- **Summer School Events**

Prayer

We have the following prayer guides that you may find useful:

- **Neighbour Fridays:** This is found in the UCB resource *Prayer for Today*, where Neighbourhood Prayer Network writes the prayers for every Friday. There is a short prayer every Friday and a prayer challenge for your street. See page 170 for details.

- **Neighbourhood Prayer Triplets:** We are encouraging as many people as possible to form prayer triplets. This is a twelve-week guide that also aims to teach, in most cases letting Scripture speak for itself. We hope that prayer triplets will continue longer term and that this guide will give people confidence to pray. Please see page 98.

- **Neighbourhood Prayer Diary:** This is a weekly prayer diary produced in partnership with Tearfund. Each day has a theme with a list of people to pray for that day. See page 153.

- **Prayer Walking:** Please see the prayer-walking guide on page 162.

Care and Share

- **Summer Church Barbecue**

- **Summer School Events**

CALENDAR

SEPTEMBER

Prayer

We have the following prayer guides that you may find useful:

- **Neighbour Fridays:** This is found in the UCB resource *Prayer for Today*, where Neighbourhood Prayer Network writes the prayers for every Friday. There is a short prayer every Friday and a prayer challenge for your street. See page 170 for details.

- **Neighbourhood Prayer Triplets:** We are encouraging as many people as possible to form prayer triplets. This is a twelve-week guide that also aims to teach, in most cases letting Scripture speak for itself. We hope that prayer triplets will continue longer term and that this guide will give people confidence to pray. Please see page 98.

- **Neighbourhood Prayer Diary:** This is a weekly prayer diary produced in partnership with Tearfund. Each day has a theme with a list of people to pray for that day. See page 153.

Share

- **www.backtochurch.co.uk:** Is there a neighbour you could invite back to church?

- **Alpha:** Invite your neighbours (if you know them well and feel comfortable) to an Alpha course.

CALENDAR

OCTOBER

Prayer

We have the following prayer guides that you may find useful:

- **Neighbour Fridays:** This is found in the UCB resource *Prayer for Today*, where Neighbourhood Prayer Network writes the prayers for every Friday. There is a short prayer every Friday and a prayer challenge for your street. See page 170 for details.

- **Neighbourhood Prayer Triplets:** We are encouraging as many people as possible to form prayer triplets. This is a twelve-week guide that also aims to teach, in most cases letting Scripture speak for itself. We hope that prayer triplets will continue longer term and that this guide will give people confidence to pray. Please see page 98.

- **Neighbourhood Prayer Diary:** This is a weekly prayer diary produced in partnership with Tearfund. Each day has a theme with a list of people to pray for that day. See page 153.

- **Festival of Life**

Care

- **The Power of Saying "Thank You":** See article on page 188.

- **Alternative Halloween:** See article on page 223.

Share

- **The Book of Hope:** See article on page 222.

CALENDAR

NOVEMBER

Prayer

We have the following prayer guides that you may find useful:

- **Neighbour Fridays:** This is found in the UCB resource *Prayer for Today*, where Neighbourhood Prayer Network writes the prayers for every Friday. There is a short prayer every Friday and a prayer challenge for your street. See page 170 for details.

- **Neighbourhood Prayer Triplets:** We are encouraging as many people as possible to form prayer triplets. This is a twelve-week guide that also aims to teach, in most cases letting Scripture speak for itself. We hope that prayer triplets will continue longer term and that this guide will give people confidence to pray. Please see page 98.

- **Neighbourhood Prayer Diary:** This is a weekly prayer diary produced in partnership with Tearfund. Each day has a theme with a list of people to pray for that day. See page 153.

Care and Share

- **Operation Christmas Child:** See article on page 194.

- **Dinner4Good:** See article on page 192.

- **Tearfund and Samaritan's Purse in Partnership with Neighbourhood Prayer Network and Dinner4Good:** See article on page 198.

CALENDAR

DECEMBER

Prayer

We have the following prayer guides that you may find useful:

- **Neighbour Fridays:** This is found in the UCB resource *Prayer for Today*, where Neighbourhood Prayer Network writes the prayers for every Friday. There is a short prayer every Friday and a prayer challenge for your street. See page 170 for details.

- **Neighbourhood Prayer Triplets:** We are encouraging as many people as possible to form prayer triplets. This is a twelve-week guide that also aims to teach, in most cases letting Scripture speak for itself. We hope that prayer triplets will continue longer term and that this guide will give people confidence to pray. Please see page 98.

- **Neighbourhood Prayer Diary:** This is a weekly prayer diary produced in partnership with Tearfund. Each day has a theme with a list of people to pray for that day. See page 153.

- **Watch Night Services:** Invite your neighbour to a watch night service on 31 December.

Care

- **Christmas Cards and Presents:** Buy your neighbour a Christmas card and if you are able a small present such as chocolate.

- **Lonely Neighbours:** Can you invite a lonely neighbour around at Christmas time, if only for an hour? Or spend some time with them in their home? (This suggestion is not suitable for those under the age of eighteen, and is best done in twos.)

Share

- **Prayer Candles:** Give out candles in your neighbourhood, to let people know you are praying for them.

- **Father's Love Letter:** Hand out the Father's Love Letter.

- **Carol or Christmas Service:** Invite your neighbour to a Christmas event in your church.

A Vision of Unity: The Brides of Christ
An anonymous prophetic vision

The large hall is filled with thousands of brides, all adorned in beautiful gowns. As far as the eye can see, there are brides everywhere.

Three brides seem to come into particular focus; the first is the oldest there. Her hair is long, grey and plaited. She is extremely distinguished, and there is no mistake – all the other brides in the room are aware of her presence. The wisdom on her face distracts onlookers from her dress, beautiful as it is. She moves gracefully throughout the room.

A second bride is eye-catching, mainly because she seems so different from the rest. Her dress is reminiscent of the sixteenth century, of Tudor times.

Finally, in the midst of so many brides, comes a bride wearing a much shorter dress, much plainer, but no less beautiful, reminiscent of a dress seen in the 1960s.

As I stare down from a balcony, the multitude of brides is overwhelming. In the blink of an eye, suddenly there are no longer many, but only one. This bride is beyond beautiful: she is captivating. Her dress is adorned with individual jewels sewn into the gown. She stands at the altar awaiting her bridegroom.

Jesus appears, dressed not in traditional Western clothes, but in an outfit more familiar perhaps in Asian cultures. His hands, with wounds, start to bleed and He smears His blood over the bridal dress. Rather than making the dress ugly, His blood causes it to shine, and the bride appears all the more beautiful.

What was striking is that before the appearance of this one bride, I could not have imagined any of the brides on their own looking any more beautiful. Yet this one bride, who seemed to be all and yet one, was staggering in beauty, bringing light to the whole room. Jesus the Bridegroom is coming for one bride!

> *"Let us be glad and rejoice and give Him glory, for the marriage of the Lamb has come, and His wife has made herself ready."*
>
> *And to her it was granted to be arrayed in fine linen, clean and bright, for the fine linen is the righteous acts of the saints.*
>
> *Then he said to me, "Write: 'Blessed are those who are called to the marriage supper of the Lamb!'" And he said to me, "These are the true sayings of God."*
>
> **(Revelation 19:7–9)**

(Please also read John 17:20–23, Ephesians 5:25–27)

True unity is when we unify around God-given vision, respecting our differences and yet not compromising on our beliefs.

Available on the website:

ABC of how to put on a stadium event

Neighbourhood Prayer Network believes that stadium events are a catalyst for unity and transformation and also a boost to confidence in the church. In partnership with the Global Day of Prayer, London, we will be profiling the journey of Wembley 2012 and subsequent events. We will explain the ins and outs of how to organise larger scale events, for those who want to start the process themselves. We will update this guide with best practice as more events occur.

THE
NAT°ONAL DAY
OF PRAYER & WORSHIP

www.ndopwembley.com

GL◉BAL
DAY OF PRAYER LONDON

www.gdoplondon.com

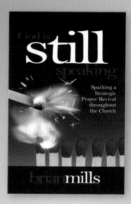
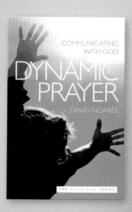
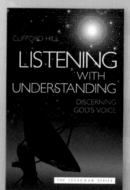

We designed...

Neighbours, Transform Your Street!

What clients say about David Lund...

"Without question one of the most creative people I have ever come across."
Graham Williams
Managing Director, Authentic (now Ragamuffin Media)

"David Lund is a creative and passionate photographer, who has a unique and rare depth of ability and versatility."
Jonathon Brown
Managing Director, Delirious Group (now Kingsway)

"Authentic Media have a long association with David Lund going back over 15 years. His book cover designs have always been of the highest quality and David will always go the extra mile in helping us find the perfect cover. I would thoroughly recommend his work!"
Malcolm Down
Head of Publishing, Authentic Media

"I have worked with David a number of times on a range of products and really appreciated his creative approach and innovative design solutions."
Simon Barker
Volunteer Ministry Team Leader

"David combines his immense creativity, design and photography into stunning promotional and marketing materials."
Karen Laister
brf, Deputy Chief Executive

"David is a highly skilled designer and photographer we have used many times. With his strong Christian faith he is very able in visually interpreting what we want to achieve."
Paul Stanier
Managing Director, Sovereign World Ltd

"David Lund's design, photography and services has always been of the highest standard, and as an orginisation have come to rely on his high level of quality in all of our promotional work."
Arthur White
Founder and Trustee of Tough Talk

"David Lund's creativity in both design and photography is incredible, GroundBreakers can't recommend him enough for his innovative ideas."
Jonathan Hulton
GroundBreakers

"I have worked with David Lund for a number of years now and he is able to turn a design brief into creative dream."
Michael Welch
Sales Manager, Scripture Union Publishing

Bring your next project to life...

Call us on **01844 204376**